Marketing Ethics

Marketing Ethics

Guidelines for Managers

Edited by
Gene R. Laczniak
Marquette University

Patrick E. Murphy
University of Notre Dame

106831

Lexington Books
D.C. Heath and Company/Lexington, Massachusetts/Toronto

Library of Congress Cataloging in Publication Data

Main entry under title:

 Marketing ethics.

 Includes index.
 1. Marketing—Addresses, essays, lectures. 2. Business ethics—Addresses, essays,
lectures. I. Laczniak, Eugene R. II. Murphy, Patrick E., 1948–
HF5415.122.M42   1985   174′ .9658   85–40107
ISBN 0-669-10833-2 (alk. paper)
ISBN 0-669-10832-4 (pbk.; alk. paper)

Third printing, August 1986
Published simultaneously in Canada
Printed in the United States of America
International Standard Book Number: 0-669-10833-2
Library of Congress Catalog Card Number: 85-40107

The paper used in this publication meets the minimum requirements of American National
Standard for Information Sciences—Permanence of Paper for Printed Library Materials,
ANSI Z39.48-1984. ∞™

Let's hear it for the boys:
Andrew and Stephen; Robert and Brendan

Contents

Figures and Tables   ix

Preface   xi

Introduction   xiii

1. Ethics in Marketing: Problems and Prospects   1
   T.R. Martin

2. Frameworks for Analyzing Marketing Ethics   9
   Gene R. Laczniak

3. Implementing and Monitoring Ethics in Advertising   27
   O.C. Ferrell

4. Studying Field Salespeople's Ethical Problems: An Approach for Designing Company Policies   41
   Alan J. Dubinsky

5. Ethical Issues in Marketing Research   55
   Donald S. Tull and *Del I. Hawkins*

6. Ethics, Price Fixing, and the Management of Price Strategy   71
   William J. Kehoe

7. Ethical Issues in Multinational Marketing   85
   David J. Fritzsche

8. Incorporating Marketing Ethics into the Organization   97
   Gene R. Laczniak and *Patrick E. Murphy*

Appendix 1:   Codes of Ethics   107

    1A: World Marketing Contact Group Marketing Creed   109

    1B: Excerpts from Caterpillar Tractor Company's Code of Worldwide Business Conduct and Operating Principles   111

    1C: Excerpts from IBM's Business Conduct Guidelines   117

    1D: Excerpts from "This We Believe," Johnson Wax Statement of Company Policy   125

    1E: Excerpts from the Johnson Wax Corporate Policy Manual: Product Advertising and Advertising Policy   129

    1F: American Advertising Federation's Code of Advertising Ethics   133

    1G: Excerpts from the ITT Code of Corporate Conduct   135

Appendix 2:   Cases   137

    2A: Heublein, Inc., A Socially Questionable Product   139

    2B: General Motors: The Engine Switch Controversy   149

    2C: Giant Food's Elimination of Item Pricing   157

    2D: The Marketing of Infant Formula in Less Developed Countries   165

Index   179

About the Contributors   183

About the Editors   185

Figures and Tables

Figures

3–1. Advertisement Illustrating an Ethical Dilemma in What Can Be Presented Tastefully in Advertising   28

3–2. Apparent Product Misrepresentation in Packaging and Promotion of M&M's Candies   31

3–3. Parody of Cigarette Ad which Discourages Smoking   34

3–4. The Two-Stage Model of Ethical/Unethical Behavior in Advertising Agencies and Corporate Advertising Departments   37

5–1. Specific Research Practices with Ethical Implications   56

5–2. Marketing Research Code of Ethics   58

5–3. Misleading Presentation of Marketing Research in Advertising Copy   60

5–4. Information to Be Included in the Research Firm's Report   67

7–1. Ethical Decision Model   92

Tables

2–1. Marketing Scenarios that Raise Ethical Questions   10

2–2. A Summary of Theoretical Commentaries on Marketing Ethics   12

4–1. Perceptions of Whether Situation Should Be Addressed by Company Policy   50

7–1. Perceptions of Ethical Standards in Marketing Provided by French, German, and American Marketers   87

8–1. Overview of Honesty and Ethical Standards   99

2A–1. Heublein, Inc. Consolidated Summary of Operations   141

2A–2. Advertising Expenditures for Distilled Spirits, 1976 Leading 10 Brands, Magazines   142

2A–3. Distilled Spirits Products, Percentage Sales Increases, 1961–1980   143

2B–1. Automobile Sales, by Selected Manufacturers   150

Preface

The overriding purpose of putting together this book is to help foster ethically and socially responsible behavior in business. When more than half the American public believes that the level of business ethics has declined significantly in the past decade, it is time for both academics and business managers to take some action. While we recognize the centrality of the business system to the human enterprise and the importance of training managers who can efficiently oversee the administration of our commercial system, we also recognize a higher order obligation. It consists of sensitizing managers to the interface of ethical values and the world of business.

Recently, major U.S. administrators of the Society of Jesus defined the goals of Jesuit higher education. This group, representing universities such as Marquette, Georgetown, Boston College, the University of San Francisco, and twenty-five others, said, "Our Jesuit purpose in professional education is to train men and women of both competence and conscience. . . . By awakening in our students the sense of values to be honored and principles to be adhered to, we can carry out the mission to influence society."* We are highly supportive and sympathetic to such a statement. We believe that the goal of a business organization is not purely the bottom line but also the use of a healthy bottom line for the good of one's fellows. Thus, without diminishing the need for the latest theoretical knowledge in the study of marketing, we believe the practice of marketing is self-actualized only when marketing strategy and tactics are tempered with a concern for the principles of justice and ethics.

This book can be used in a variety of ways. First, no current book is exclusively devoted to the topic of marketing ethics. However, increasing concern is being focused on business ethics generally and marketing ethics specifically. In fact, numerous articles have appeared in significant business

---

*This definition of the goals of Jesuit education is quoted from a speech by Marquette University President John P. Raynor, at the dedication of the College of Business Administration Building, December 2, 1984.

journals such as the *Harvard Business Review*, the *California Management Review*, and *Business Horizons*. In addition, business periodicals such as the *Wall Street Journal* and *Business Week* have often dealt with the ethical and moral shortcomings of corporate and marketing managers.

We believe several distinguishing features make this book notable. First, for those concerned with gaining exposure to the issues in marketing with major ethical dimensions, the chapters cover the main areas of concern within the jurisdiction of marketing ethics. Included are the topics of, among others, advertising ethics, sales management ethics, multinational marketing, and marketing research ethics. Also found are the reprints of several organizational codes of ethics, excerpting in particular the marketing dimensions of these codes. Third, each article concludes with some specific guidelines for management. These guidelines involve steps that managers might take to improve or monitor ethical concerns in their organization.

In conclusion, we acknowledge that this book was made possible only by the generous contributions of the time, effort, and monies of several individuals and organizations. First and foremost, we thank our colleagues who contributed the chapters that comprise this book. Their writings in marketing ethics have been the result of a strong value commitment since marketing ethics has hardly been a mainstream or appreciated research area in the field of marketing. Next, we acknowledge the financial support of the Scholl Foundation for providing the money to initiate the conference upon which this book is based. In addition, we recognize the philosophical and organizational support of Dr. Thomas A. Bausch, dean, and Dr. Ralph E. Brownlee, director of special projects, at the College of Business Administration, Marquette University. We also thank Sheila Fessenbecker, Joanne Riepe, and Jane Gray, who worked so diligently and gave so generously of their time in the typing, editing, and administration of the materials in the book. Last, we salute the many honest, ethical, and hard-working marketing managers everywhere whose reputation is besmirched by the unethical actions of a few.

Introduction

The ethical sensitivity of all professionals—lawyers, physicians, educators, and business executives—has come under close scrutiny in recent years. Post-Watergate morality has dictated that the past level of ethics exhibited by professionals is no longer adequate and perhaps never was. This renewed ethical concern represents the reoccurrence of an established issue: the lack of ethical behavior exhibited by many persons in positions of responsibility.

Within the business firm, the functional area most closely related to ethical abuse is marketing. This is because marketing is the function of business charged with communicating and openly satisfying customers. Thus, marketing is closest to the public view and, consequently, is subject to considerable societal analysis and scrutiny.

Recent events have indicated that the ethics of individuals and organizations involved in marketing have been widely debated. Questions of propriety have arisen in areas such as advertising, personal selling, pricing, and international operations. These topics can represent strategic decision areas in an organization. As is discussed later, many persons believe marketing to be the area of business most prone to unethical practices. Furthermore, among the marketing-related positions that have come under scrutiny for unethical practices are those of sales representative, product manager, advertising executive, market research manager, and physical distribution manager. Thus, social pressures increasingly dictate that marketers examine their dealings with consumers, competitors, suppliers, and the government. At present, executives are looking for mechanisms to help them better scrutinize some of the ethical issues facing their organization and make the necessary adjustments so their operations will perform consistently with their social responsibilities.

Because of the growing necessity of marketers to examine their ethical responsibilities, a compendium of recent articles on the issue of marketing ethics which include specific managerial guidelines has been compiled. This set of articles (with two exceptions) is drawn from a conference on the topic of marketing ethics that was held in summer 1983 at Marquette University and was made possible by a grant of the Scholl Foundation. We believe this book of readings keenly examines the area of marketing ethics and suggests institutional arrangements and adaptations that can help organizations cope with ethical problems in marketing.

The book is primarily intended for thoughtful, practicing managers who are interested in the ethical issues surrounding marketing as well as for seminar-type graduate courses in marketing ethics. The chapters contain references to the academic literature that should also be of interest to the business ethics scholar. These references provide guidance for those scholars wishing to do additional reading in the area of marketing ethics. However, the pragmatic tone of the chapters is also substantial enough that each should be of reasonable practical use to the problem-oriented manager.

In chapter 1, T.R. Martin provides the foundation for the chapters that follow. Martin views marketing ethics as a subheading of the general issue of business ethics. The chapter delineates why all businesspeople should be concerned about ethics and what some of the major difficulties are in maintaining an ethical demeanor. Martin then makes a compelling case for why additional discussion and research are needed in the area of marketing ethics.

In chapter 2, Gene R. Laczniak discusses three ethical frameworks drawn from moral philosophy that can help bring insight into marketing decision making. The frameworks are not intended to provide the only ethical answer but to help marketing managers better systematize their thinking when dealing with marketing problems that have ethical implications. The major thrust of the chapter is to provide managers with a philosophical background to discuss marketing ethics more intelligently.

Chapter 3 is contributed by O.C. Ferrell. The topic of this chapter, advertising, is among the most ethically charged issues of marketing ethics. The chapter is built around three questions important to the analysis of ethics in the practice of advertising. First, is advertising by its very nature unethical? Ferrell discusses this question and concludes that in general advertising is a sound ethical and moral practice. The second question deals with how organizational dynamics influence ethically related decisions in advertising. After examining several streams of evidence, Ferrell concludes that middle-management-level marketers are the keepers of organizational values rather than top management. Third, the chapter examines what should be done to maintain and, if necessary, improve ethical conduct in advertising. A specific set of questions that will help managers evaluate their current and future situation regarding ethical advertising is provided in the form of managerial guidelines.

In chapter 4, Alan J. Dubinsky provides a pragmatic approach for resolving the ethical conflicts of sales personnel. The chapter describes some of the major problems with ethical situations that face sales personnel. It also provides a detailed and operational set of guidelines for establishing, through research, what are the most troublesome ethical situations that face the sales force of a particular company.

Chapter 5, contributed by Donald S. Tull and Del I. Hawkins, reviews the major ethical questions that derive from one of the most sensitive areas of marketing practice—marketing research. Included in this presentation are the ethical research code of the American Marketing Association as well as a discussion of the major ethical issues that affect the public, clients, respondents, and practioners. Benefits of taking an ethical approach to marketing research are also articulated.

In chapter 6, William J. Kehoe provides some thoughts on the ethical dimensions of pricing. He argues that pricing is among the most difficult areas to assess fairly because of the problematic nature of establishing what is a just price. Kehoe delineates specific areas of pricing that have raised ethical concern and provides a special focus on the area of price fixing. The chapter concludes by providing managerial guidelines which deal with questionable pricing strategies that might infringe upon the employee, the market, corporation, and the consumer.

In chapter 7, David Fritzsche examines ethics as it particularly applies to the multinational corporation. Included here is a summary report of the perceptions of marketers of France, Germany, and the United States concerning the prevalent value ethic that dominates these countries. Finally, three ethical principles are incorporated into a decision-making model that can help managers operating in the international arena to resolve ethical conflicts.

The concluding chapter, contributed by Gene R. Laczniak and Patrick E. Murphy, provides specific organizational mechanisms that might be utilized to implement improved marketing ethics. Discussed are the utility of having marketing codes of conduct, the value of marketing ethics committees, and the feasibility of providing educational modules (dealing with ethics) for marketing management. Finally, the potential role of the vice-president of marketing in helping to create a climate of morality and supporting behavior within the organization is discussed.

Appendix material includes abridged reprints of the organizational code of conduct of several large corporations as well as a few case studies that may generate debate among those who utilize this book for educational seminars as well as to stimulate policy discussion. In the final analysis, the authors hope that this book contributes in some measure to the discussion of marketing ethics within organizations. It has been our experience that only when members of an organization become sensitive to the potential ethical implications of their actions is the organization moved to take steps that could meaningfully improve the moral climate within that organization.

1
Ethics in Marketing: Problems and Prospects

T.R. Martin

T he subject of ethics in marketing can be viewed as a subheading of ethics in business. Most of what is said in this chapter is addressed to the more general subject. Particular cases involving marketing aspects such as product safety, truth in advertising, price conspiracies, and bribery certainly merit our attention, but they are left for discussion by others. Clearly, however, as one makes a case for scrutinizing the ethics of business, the same reasoning applies to marketing as a specific manifestation of business practice.

Why Worry about Ethics?

Although the answer to this question might be rather obvious, we probably should ask explicitly why we should even concern ourselves with ethics in business. We can each answer for ourselves. It is fair to say, however, that most people want a just (or good) society. One fundamental characteristic of such a good society is that justice and charity prevail therein. Ethics and justice are almost synonymous. The whole world longs for both, especially in the international order. But humans being human, the good society, in which justice and charity reign supreme, is an elusive goal—an unattainable goal if we expect perfection. Our task, though, is to fight for it, never to acquiesce in evil. If we consider ourselves good men and women, we must take on the responsibility of helping all society to seek to perfect itself, starting with perfecting ourselves.

A second reason for concerning ourselves with business ethics is less lofty but nevertheless worthy. We live perforce in an economic system. In the United States, we have historically been dedicated to private enterprise, free markets, competition, and government by law. At the root of this dedication is our passionate belief in and desire for freedom. (In case we tend to think that there can hardly be an exception taken to such values, let us note that private enterprise is not the norm throughout the world.) Such a system can endure only if it operates in such a way that the majority believe that justice does prevail in it. If it lacks legitimacy, the system will likely fail.

The results of polls addressed to people's perceptions of the institution of business are not assuring. There is a vast amount of skepticism and cynicism toward business, as indicated by a Gallup Poll (1983) that listed several marketing occupations near the bottom of the ethics ladder. Perhaps it would be more accurate to say people are more skeptical toward individual managers rather than business. There still appears to be an abiding faith in private enterprise as a concept or ideology. Also, a great lack of faith is expressed in the managers who run it. Whether or not the facts are correctly seen, this perception should be a grave concern.

Governments have responded to the call for more control of business—to force more justice into it. Witness the flood of legislation since 1960 in the consumer area alone (for a summary, see Feldman 1980). Business people frequently castigate the bureaucrats and legislators who foist off all the new rules on the commercial sector. There is even a name for the archetype villain; the regulators have become the *new class*. But in the absence of popular outcry and support, what Steiner and Steiner (1980) call the fundamental redefinition of capitalism would not have come about.

Achieving a just society by writing more laws, creating more commissions and regulatory agencies, however, is probably a chimera. A society is just to the extent its people are just—not, as some seem to believe, to the extent it has mountains of laws and regulations written by skillful lawyers. In the long run, unethical behavior in business could threaten the system, threaten to destroy freedom—not cataclysmically but by inches. And that would be a great tragedy, would it not?

Difficulties in Dealing with Ethics

Ethics is one of those subjects that seem to become more perplexing the more one explores it. The various schools of thought such as utilitarianism and egoism add up to a considerable amount of confusion for most of us. Some principles would find general agreement, and there are some rules to which most ethicists—and most nonethicists, for that matter—would subscribe. There is a consensus that lying, stealing, cheating, and murder, for example, are wrong. However, observe the difficulties that arise in applying principles to subjects such as nuclear weapons and abortion. Consensus is not reached so easily here. Epstein (1981) has pointed out, "As students of Jewish law are fully aware . . . the seemingly clear and precise Ten Commandments have generated, over the period of those millennia, literally millions of pages of Rabbinic commentary and interpretation arising out of case-by-case application of Mosaic law to specific factual circumstances."

All the lack of certitude means that ethics in business or any other activity does not lend itself to simple analyses, but for purposes of discussion, let us imagine that a marketer is faced with a problem that poses an ethical question. Let us assume there is a correct answer, which may be defined as one with which the great majority of ethicists would agree. Now look at four possibilities for the marketer. First, he or she could agree with the ethicists and comply with their judgment. Second, he or she could agree with the ethicists but decide to do the unethical thing in spite of that agreement. Third, the marketer could misanalyze the situation (believing his or her choice to be moral) and decide to do the unethical thing, in which case we could say the marketer is acting ethically in the subjective sense. Last, the marketer could tend to analyze correctly but finally rationalize so that he or she is convinced that what the ethicists would say is unethical is ethical or excusable for this person. (As someone once said, "I wrestled with my conscience—and I won!")

Dealing with the three different ways in which our marketer could reach the wrong decision would likely require three different approaches. In the second illustration, for example, the marketer is a criminal—correctly analyzing, deciding to do wrong. This person needs to be made to see that crime does not pay. The third could not correctly analyze the situation; this person needs instruction in ethics. The fourth, the rationalizer, is the slippery one. Many of us can probably see ourselves in this person at one time or another. He or she needs to learn to be honest with him- or herself. However, precisely how to teach that honesty is a major question.

The Prevailing Ethos

Which of these three unethical scenarios accounts for most of the improper behavior in business? The likeliest candidate is probably the rationalization model. There are crooks, to be sure, but penologists tell us that almost every penitentiary inmate believes he got a "bum rap." Some people can hardly tell the difference between right and wrong, and in many situations the right answer is not readily apparent. (There are also situations in which good, professional ethicists would disagree, but this case was ruled out of the illustration.) Case histories suggest that the problem with which we should be most concerned is the rationalizer. It is so easy to rationalize. Even the executioners in the Holocaust could defend themselves for "just following orders."

Marshall B. Clinard (1983), professor emeritus of sociology at the University of Wisconsin-Madison, completed a survey of sixty-four retired corporate middle managers from Fortune 500 companies. As reported in the *Wall Street Journal* (Ricklefs 1983), "only about one in four said they would report price-fixing or illegal kickbacks." Some of the comments are interesting: "Price-fixing involves money and not people's safety or the national interest. . . . it would be disloyal to the corporation." "We might lose business if we didn't give illegal rebates and kickbacks."

Another *Wall Street Journal* article (May 25, 1983), titled "Building Costs on Highways Are Declining," is quite instructive:

> One big reason for the lower prices: Justice Department prosecutions of widespread bid-rigging by highway contractors. . . . Since 1979, criminal grand juries in 21 states have investigated highway bid-fixing. Prosecutions in 15 of those states have produced indictments of more than 180 companies and 200 executives. Convictions have led to fines totaling $41 million and numerous jail sentences.
>
> The Transportation Department's inspector general, who has aided the investigations, recently reported "a strong correlation" in contractor bidding patterns "between the success of our activity and the reduction in bid prices."
>
> Richard Braun, a Justice Department attorney who prosecuted cases in five states, says bid-rigging was "pervasive" in each of them.
>
> The practice was a "way of life" for years in Tennessee and other states, officials say. "The asphalt people just took it for granted. Most of them didn't even think it was breaking the law—it was more or less helping each other out," says Samuel Slate of Virginia's Highways and Transportation Department.
>
> As one of the characters in *The Mikado* says, "Here's a pretty mess."
> [p. 1]

Studies such as Clinard's (1983) are most informative. And there have been others. A quick perusal of the business press shows that hardly a day goes by without a report of some kind of shenanigan in high business places. Nevertheless, there is a great deal we do not know about unethical behavior in business. Business managers often refer to a "few rotten apples in the barrel" because the number of reported cases is small relative to the size of the business universe. But one of the interviewers in Clinard's project said that giving illegal rebates and kickbacks "is a fairly common corporate practice in my industry." After the many disclosures of overseas payoffs in the mid-1970s, the chairman of the Securities and Exchange Commission (SEC) said, "This is bribery, influence peddling, and corruption on a scale I never dreamed existed ("How Clean Is Business?" 1975). So have we a few rotten apples—or the tip of an iceberg?

On the subject of the prevailing ethos, we can detect another trend in our litigious society. In brief it is, If something is legal, it is fine; that is, the important question becomes, is it legal? The other question—Is it ethical?—often suffers the indignity of not even being asked. Legal considerations crowd out the ethical. If this is true, it is most unfortunate. Surely, it is obvious that legal is not synonymous with ethical. Furthermore, the question of legality tends to degenerate into a very base one: Can we get away with it? Almost every large corporation in this country has a legal staff and frequently consults outside personnel. Only a tiny few have even one ethicist on their staffs, and even fewer would find it advisable to consult a professional ethicist outside their organization.

These questions prompt a hypothesis. We hear much these days about the culture of business firms. Someone said that there are 164 definitions of culture. However, the word is fairly suitable for the notion offered here, which is that business as an institution has an ethos of its own wherein behavior that most of us would call unethical is too often tolerated or even sanctioned. Too often when the respectable business manager arrives at work in the morning, he or she puts on a different hat, leaves civilization, and enters the jungle. The manager rationalizes many times in many ways. Business then becomes a subculture: It is not representative of the larger culture. The business manager lives in both.

Of course, many firms and businesspeople do not fit into the subculture model suggested here. But is it not true that business has many customs that do not square well with society's notions of what constitutes justice?

The Need for Research and Discussion of Ethics

The hypothesis suggested points to another proposition: We do not know as much as we should about the ethical climate in business. Whatever our perceptions are (and they range from very good to very bad), they are not well supported by solid research. This is not to denigrate the good work of some of our colleagues, from Baumhart (1961) to the aforementioned study by Clinard (1983). We do have bits of information and insights, but out knowledge is rather skimpy. The sum of the work that has been done in the area is not large.

Why is it that more has not been done to probe into the realities of what goes on and why? One answer might be that this kind of research is very difficult to conduct. Business managers are often reluctant to talk, to disclose practices that might raise questions, to bare their souls because the area is very sensitive.

Another possible reason for the paucity of research is that business has hardly rushed to support it. Business's interest may be measured in part by the kind and amount of support it provides to investigate the subject. There has been some, but on the whole, the support is small.

If we buy into the proposition that the welfare of the United States depends in an important way on the ethical climate in business, some new research efforts should be mounted. Business and academicians should cooperate in some innovative exploration into the subject—academicians because they have the interest and skills, business because it has the laboratories and funds. For example, a major study of marketing ethics could be funded by one of the large packaged goods firms.

The significance of the subculture idea is this. If the ethical climate in business is and is destined to be simply a mirror image of the ethical climate in society as a whole, then its deficiencies may best be reduced by attacking society's wrong values; if, conversely, the ethical climate in business is peculiar to business—if there is something about the environment of business that makes business an ethical jungle—we should attack that segment specifically. We should use tactical rather than strategic weapons, if you will. But first we have to know the kind of target with which we are dealing and where it is. For instance, many of the questions posed in this chapter need to be empirically studied.

Is ethics in business worth the effort? Herman, in his book *Corporate Control, Corporate Power* (1981), has this to say: "We may be approaching full circle in the West . . . to the present stage of evolution where economic freedom has produced an environment dominated by vast, impersonal organizations . . . that respond only to material incentives" (p. 301). If this is true, we should certainly do all we can to reverse the trend.

Teaching Ethics

For those on university faculties, it would be appropriate to mention the matter of teaching ethics in our business schools. Those who watch the literature know that there have been research efforts directed to the question of whether ethics can even be taught. Miller and Miller (1976), for example, entitled their research, "It's Too Late for Ethics Courses in Business Schools." No less an authority than Drucker (1981) takes a very negative view toward courses in business ethics.

In contrast is the perspective of Reverend Oliver F. Williams, who is on the management faculty at Notre Dame:

> There is no "quick fix" for fashioning moral persons. A course or two in business ethics . . . can provide some assistance in the recognition of the ethical dimension of business problems and their analysis and resolution. However, these courses all presuppose a basically moral person. Character traits such as loyalty, sensitivity, justice, compassion, and honesty may be reinforced in an academic course but they surely do not originate there. Courses in business ethics in undergraduate and MBA programs, or in the business setting, are essential. These courses are no substitute for caring and loving parents early in one's development or for a wholesome community in our schools and work places. [1982, p. 22]

We should not give up teaching the subject, but we probably need to examine more systematically how we are doing it and assess what the effects really are. Williams quoted from one participant in an ethics training program at Cummins Engine Company as follows: "My MBA program never touched on ethical issues, and the workshop filled an important need for me." That statement is a serious indictment of his school's MBA program. Incidentally, if the statement is true and the school in question was accredited by the American Assembly of Collegiate Schools of Business, the school was violating accreditation standards.

The Future

We all want to see improvement in the ethical climate in business. We are not interested in the subject only clinically. How does the future look?

Hardly a day passes without a report in the business press of some kind of questionable business conduct—an indictment, a court judgment of guilt, a grand jury investigation, or the like. From this one could gain an impression that the business world is indeed a dirty place. It's dirty enough, all right. But there are some good things going on too.

An increasing number of schools are teaching business ethics, and an increasing number of professors are doing research in the subject. Nothing will happen overnight, but something worthwhile should come from the efforts of the academicians. An increasing number of companies are forming board committees with the title "Committee on Social Responsibility" or some such. A growing number of companies are putting on in-house programs in ethics for their managers. A few companies have resident ethicists on their staffs.

One of the most encouraging developments is a heightened interest in business ethics on the part of top management. Some highly placed executives are coming out from behind the corporate veil and speaking publicly on the necessity of practicing good ethics. These people are the key. We know that institutionalization is a slow but essential process. If the people at the top do not have the conviction or the determination to make their organizations practice good ethics, nothing will happen. They also, of course, have to know how to go about the process. There is a long way to go, perhaps, but help is on the way.

References

Baumhart, Raymond C. 1961. "How Ethical Are Businessmen?" *Harvard Business Review* (July-August), p. 156.

"Building Costs on Highways Declining," 1983. *Wall Street Journal* (May 25), p. 1.

Clinard, Marshall B. 1983. *Corporate Ethics and Crime: The Role of Middle Management.* Beverly Hills: Sage Publications.

Drucker, Peter F. 1981. "What Is 'Business Ethics'?" *The Public Interest* 63 (Spring), p. 18.

Epstein, Edwin M. 1981. "Defining Corporate Social Responsibility." In *Private Enterprise and Public Purpose*, P. Sethi and C. Swanson, eds. New York: John Wiley & Sons, p. 91.

Feldman, Lawrence P. 1980. *Consumer Protection: Problems and Prospects*, 2nd ed. St. Paul: West Publishing Co.

Gallup Poll. 1983. "Honesty and Ethical Standards," *Report No. 214* (July).

Herman, Edward S. 1981. *Corporate Control, Corporate Power*. New York: Cambridge University Press, p. 301.

"How Clean Is Business?" 1975. *Newsweek*, September 1, p. 50.

Miller, Mary S., and Edward A. Miller. 1976. "It's Too Late for Ethics Courses in Business Schools." *Business and Society Review* (Spring), p. 40.

Ricklefs, Roger. 1983. "Gallup Poll/WSJ Survey," *The Wall Street Journal*, October 31, November 1, November 2, Section 2.

Steiner, George, and John Steiner. 1980. *Business, Government & Society*. New York: Random House, p. 21.

Williams, Oliver F. 1982. "Business Ethics: A Trojan Horse?" *California Management Review* (Summer), p. 22.

2
Frameworks for Analyzing Marketing Ethics

Gene R. Laczniak

The issue of ethics in marketing is a concern for marketing practitioners, educators, and researchers. Virtually every business manager would agree that ethical implications are often inherent in marketing decisions. Particularly perplexing are some of the tough-question situations that can occur in which the degree of moral culpability in a specific case is subject to debate. Table 2–1 presents a few illustrations of such situations. The scenarios should be reviewed at this time since they will be used to illustrate various theoretical points made later in the chapter. The situations described in these scenarios deal with the areas of distribution/retailing, promotion, product management, pricing, and nonbusiness marketing. Thus, almost every area of marketing strategy can pose serious ethical questions.

Over the years, marketing writers have tried to address some of the ethical concerns stemming from the practice of marketing. A literature review on the topic of marketing ethics (Murphy and Laczniak 1981) identified and discussed nearly 100 articles, papers, and books that include commentary related to specific ethical dimensions of marketing. Unfortunately, while the various writings contained many provocative suggestions, as well as some interesting insights, they were seldom based on an underlying theory or framework of marketing ethics. Most often, the writings pointed out existing ethical abuses (Rudelius and Bucholz 1979), reported managerial perceptions of ethical behavior (Sturdivant and Cocanougher 1973; Ferrell and Weaver 1978), or provided some rudimentary suggestions for improving ethics (Kelley 1969; Kizilbash et al. 1979). A few marketing academics have tried to take a more global approach to the ethics issue (see table 2–2 for a summary), but even these writings, taken as a whole, have lacked sophisticated theoretical foundations. Normally, references to ethical theories or decision rules have been limited to the citation of simple ethical maxims. Typical of these thumbnail ethical maxims are the following:

Reprinted from *Journal of Macromarketing*, Spring 1983, pp. 7–18.

The golden rule: Act in the way you would expect others to act toward you.

The utilitarian principle: Act in a way that results in the greatest good for the greatest number.

Kant's categorical imperative: Act in such a way that the action taken under the circumstances could be a universal law or rule of behavior.

The professional ethic: Take only actions that would be viewed as proper by a disinterested panel of professional colleagues.

The TV test: A manager should always ask, "Would I feel comfortable explaining to a national TV audience why I took this action?"

While not without value, these limited ethical frameworks have hampered the analysis of ethics by marketing managers. They have also caused marketing educators some discomfort when discussing ethical issues in the classroom. In short, many marketing educators have shied away from lecturing on the topic of marketing ethics because of the perception that existing frameworks for analyzing the topic are simplistic and lack theoretical rigor. The net result is that the seeming absence of theoretical frameworks for ethical decision making has retarded the teaching, practice, and research of marketing ethics.

This chapter presents some existing ethical frameworks that go beyond ethical maxims in their detail. These frameworks are likely to be useful in stimulating marketing ethics research, establishing a background for discussion of ethical issues in the classroom, and perhaps providing guidance for ethical decision making by marketing managers. The frameworks discussed have no magical monopoly on moral propriety; they are presented with the hope that they might engender additional ethical sensitivity among marketing academics, students, researchers, and managers.

Table 2–1
Marketing Scenarios that Raise Ethical Questions

Scenario 1

The Thrifty Supermarket chain has 12 stores in the City of Gotham, U.S.A. The company's policy is to maintain the same prices for all items at all stores. However, the distribution manager knowingly sends the poorest cuts of meat and the lowest quality produce to the store located in the low-income section of town. He justifies this action based on the fact that this store has the highest overhead due to factors such as employee turnover, pilferage, and vandalism. Is the distribution manager's economic rationale sufficient justification for his allocation method?

Scenario 2

The Independent Chevy Dealers of Metropolis, U.S.A. have undertaken an advertising campaign headlined by the slogan: "Is your family's life worth 45 MPG?"

Table 2-1 continued

The ads admit that while Chevy subcompacts are not as fuel efficient as foreign imports and cost more to maintain, they are safer according to government-sponsored crash tests. The ads implicitly ask if responsible parents, when purchasing a car, should trade off fuel efficiency for safety. Is it ethical for the dealers' association to use a fear appeal to offset an economic disadvantage?

Scenario 3

A few recent studies have linked the presence of the artificial sweetener "subsugural" to cancer in laboratory rats. While the validity of these findings has been hotly debated by medical experts, the Food and Drug Administration has ordered products containing the ingredient banned from sale in the United States. The Jones Company sends all its sugar-free J.C. Cola (which contains subsugural) to European supermarkets because the sweetener has not been banned there. Is it acceptable for the Jones Company to send an arguably unsafe product to another market without waiting for further evidence?

Scenario 4

The Acme Companys sells industrial supplies through its own sales force that calls on company purchasing agents. Acme has found that providing the purchasing agent with small gifts helps cement a cordial relationship and creates goodwill. Acme follows the policy: the bigger the order, the bigger the gift to the purchasing agent. The gifts range from a pair of tickets to a sporting event to outboard motors and snowmobiles. Acme does not give gifts to personnel at companies they know have an explicit policy prohibiting the acceptance of such gifts. Assuming no laws are violated, is Acme's policy of providing gifts to purchasing agents morally proper?

Scenario 5

The Buy American Electronics Co. has been selling its highly rated System X Color television sets (21″, 19″, 12″) for $700, $500, and $300 respectively. These prices have been relatively uncompetitive in the market. After some study, Buy American substitutes several cheaper components (which engineering says may reduce the quality of performance slightly) and passes on the savings to the consumer in the form of a $100 price reduction on each model. Buy American institutes a price-oriented promotional campaign that neglects to mention that the second generation System X sets are different from the first. Is the company's competitive strategy ethical?

Scenario 6

The Smith and Smith Advertising Agency has been struggling financially. Mr. Smith is approached by the representative of a small South American country that is on good terms with the U.S. Department of State. He wants S and S to create a multi-million dollar advertising and public relations campaign to bolster the image of the country and increase the likelihood that it will receive U.S. foreign aid assistance and attract investment capital. Smith knows the country is a dictatorship that has been accused of numerous human rights violations. Is it ethical for the Smith and Smith Agency to undertake the proposed campaign?

Adapted from Patrick E. Murphy and Gene R. Laczniak, "Marketing Ethics: A Review with Implications for Managers, Educators and Researchers," in B. Enis and K. Roering, eds., *Review of Marketing 1981* (Chicago: American Marketing Association), p. 251.

Table 2–2
A Summary of Theoretical Commentaries on Marketing Ethics

Author/Year	Theme
Walton (1961)	Ethical standards of marketers are below par; however, society in general suffers from low moral standards.
Aldersòn (1964)	Personal morality is constrained by organizational and ecological factors.
Patterson (1966)	Operational guidelines are lacking for the ethical prescriptions postulated by organizations. More checks and balances needed.
McMahon (1967)	A condemnation of situational ethics is presented.
Farmer (1967)	The public perceives the field of marketing as hucksterism.
Bartels (1967) .	Various external factors on ethical behavior, such as culture and the given economic environment, are identified.
Westing (1967)	Personal morality is the dominant factor in most ethical decisions. Ethics exists above the law, which regulates the lowest common demoninator of expected behavior.
Colihan (1967)	Consumer pressure will dictate marketing's ethics in years to come.
Pruden (1971)	Personal, organizational, and professional ethics interact to influence decision making; sometimes they can conflict.
Steiner (1976)	Marketers are perceived as unethical because of an inability of the public to perceive the value of the time, place, and possession utility provided by marketing.
Farmer (1977)	Marketing will never be perceived as ethical because fundamentally it is persuasion.
Murphy, Laczniak, and Lusch (1978)	Organizational adjustments to insure ethical marketing are discussed.
Robin (1980)	The acceptance of relativist philosophy can alleviate ethical conflicts in marketing.

For a more detailed discussion, see Patrick E. Murphy and Gene R. Laczniak, "Marketing Ethics: A Review with Implications for Managers, Educators and Researchers," in B. Enis and K. Roering, eds., *Review of Marketing 1981* (Chicago: American Marketing Association), pp. 251–266.

Frameworks versus Theories

Some readers will undoubtedly be concerned whether the following viewpoints reflecting ethics should properly be designated as theories, frameworks, propositions, or some other metaphysical specification. Rawls (1971), whose perspective is examined, characterizes his work as a theory, and it is accepted as such by most moral philosophers. In contrast, if one uses the definition of theory utilized by Hunt (1976, p. 104), the work of Rawls might not qualify as a theory because of its normative nature and the fact that it is derived from an idealization that is not reflective of the real world.

Others such as Fisk (1982, p. 5), view a framework as being broader than a theory and therefore more akin to a general paradigm that can accommodate several consistent or contrasting theories. For example, the life-cycle framework has spawned a variety of life-cycle-inspired theories. On this basis, deeming the ethical viewpoints described in the following as frameworks would be incorrect because they are somewhat narrower in scope.

Since all marketers would fail to agree that the opinions expressed here about ethics are either frameworks or theories, I am in a dilemma. Clearly the viewpoints are, at minimum, "skeletal structures designed to support a perspective"—in this case, a perspective about ethics. Since this conforms to the dictionary definition of *framework*, I use that terminology and offer my apologies in advance to those philosophers of science who subscribe to a lexicon more linguistically precise than mine.

Rationale for the Frameworks

Ethical frameworks have been developed by William David Ross, Thomas Garrett, and John Rawls. Their paradigms have been selected for discussion here because they are multidimensional, nonutilitarian in nature and significant in some important fashion.

Multidimensional

One of the impediments that has limited the study of marketing ethics in the classroom is the perception by many business educators that existing guidelines for ethical behavior are simplistic. This viewpoint has considerable validity. For example, what precisely is the value of the golden rule in assessing whether a firm should pay some bribe money to retain a lucrative foreign contract? The usefulness of such a maxim clearly is limited. One value of the three frameworks selected for presentation is that they illustrate that ethical frameworks do exist that go well beyond the frailty of a maxim in their sophistication; that is, some ethical theories attempt to specify multidimensional factors for consideration.

Nonutilitarian in Nature

In the main, much of the theoretical thinking about marketing ethics has been implicitly based on utilitarian theory. Utilitarianism holds that actions should be judged primarily upon whether they produce the greatest good for the greatest number. Utilitarianism is based historically on the well-known writings of Jeremy Bentham and John Stuart Mill. Many of the ethical defenses for the efficiency of the free market have also been rooted in utilitarianism. Typically, the argument revolves around showing how free market capitalism benefits a greater number of persons than controlled systems. There are many articulate, modern day spokespersons for utilitarianism (Sartorius 1975; Singer 1976). However, generally speaking, utilitarian analysis has been subjected to a large amount of criticism (Beauchamp and Bowie 1979). The crux of the objection to utilitarianism lies in the fact that a desirable end may come about because of an unjust means. Thus, many moral philosophers have turned their attention to nonutilitarian theories that emphasize the process of arriving at outcomes as much as the outcome. Because of the relative familiarity of business managers with utilitarian thinking and the currency of examining other alternatives, the three frameworks highlighted here are nonutilitarian.

Significant

Each of the frameworks selected for explication is theoretically important for some reason. Ross (1930) was one of the first philosophers to try to specify a list of the major ethical responsibilities facing any person. In addition, Ross tried to create a paradigm that would be a supplement to rather than a replacement for utilitarian thinking. Garrett (1966), in contrast, tried to take various streams of ethical thought and blend them in a fashion that would be useful to the practicing business manager. Thus, the major contribution of the Garrett work is its pragmatic orientation. Finally, the Rawls theory (1971) is the most talked about work on ethics in recent years. Rawls's writings have had an enormous influence on moral philosophy in the 1970s, and this impact is reflected in current writings on the topic of ethics.

The Prima Facie Duties Framework

In his theory of moral philosophy, Englishman William David Ross tried to combine the underpinnings of utilitarianism with certain aspects of Kantian philosophical theory. The bulk of the Ross (1930) model is the notion that there are several prima facie (at first sight) duties that, under most circumstances, constitute moral obligations. Ross contends that these prima facie duties are self-evident (p. 29) in the sense that persons of sufficient mental maturity will recognize that there are certain acts they ought to do. Ross (p. 21) postulated six categories of prima facie duties:

1. *Duties of fidelity* stem from previous actions that have been taken. These would include (to name a few) the duty to remain faithful to contracts,

to keep promises, to tell the truth, and to redress wrongful acts. In a marketing context, this might include conducting all the quality and safety testing that has been promised consumers, maintaining a rigorous warranty/servicing program, and refraining from deceptive or misleading promotional campaigns. For example, in scenario 2 of table 2–1, the dealers' association may decide that the heavy-handed fear appeal is in bad taste because of the implicit duty of fidelity they have to potential auto buyers.

2. *Duties of gratitude* are rooted in acts other persons have taken toward the person or organization under focus. This usually means that a special obligation exists between relatives, friends, partners, cohorts, and so forth. In a marketing context, this might mean retaining an ad agency a while longer because it has rendered meritorious service for several years or extending extra credit to a historically special customer who is experiencing a cash flow problem. In scenario 4 of table 2–1, Acme management may conclude that the duty of gratitude would allow the provision of a small gift if such a practice is not explicitly forbidden by the client organization.

3. *Duties of justice* are based on the obligation to distribute rewards based on merit. The justice referred to here is justice beyond the letter of the law. For example, an organization using sealed-bid purchasing to secure services should award the contract according to procedure rather than allow the second or third lowest bidder to rebid. Or in scenario 1 of table 2–1, the distribution manager might reason that the managerial problems caused by a few shoplifting or troublemaking customers is not a sufficient reason to discriminate against all the store's buyers.

4. *Duties of beneficence* rest on the notion that actions taken can improve the intelligence, virtue, or happiness of others. Basically, this is the obligation to do good, if a person has the opportunity. In scenario 6 of table 2–1, this might mean that the Smith and Smith Agency turns down the public relations contract, albeit financially attractive, because of the duty to support the human rights of others.

5. *Duties of self-improvement* reside in the concept that actions should be taken to improve our personal virtue, intelligence, or happiness. This seems to represent a modified restatement of moral egoism: Act in a way that will promote one's self-interest. In a marketing context, this might justify a manager's attempting to maximize the return on investment (ROI) of his profit center because such performance may lead to pay increases and organizational promotion. In scenario 6 of table 2–1, this might mean that Smith and Smith undertakes the public relations (PR) contract to survive because, after all, the charges against the client country have not been proven, and the country's government is officially recognized by the U.S. Department of State.

6. *Duties of nonmaleficence (noninjury)* consist of duties not to injure others. In a marketing context, this might involve doing the utmost to

insure product safety, providing adequate information to enable consumers to use the products they purchase properly, and refraining from coercive tactics when managing a channel of distribution. For example, in scenario 3 of table 2–1, Jones Co. may decide against exporting the controversial soft drinks to maximize consumer safety, even though it believes the government's data are invalid.

Several additional comments about these duties are in order. First, Ross (1930) did not intend his six duties to constitute a comprehensive code of ethics. Rather, he believed that the list represented several moral obligations that persons incurred above and beyond the law. Thus, if a person recognized a prima facie duty, a moral obligation existed that might mandate specific ethical action.

How does one recognize when a prima facie duty is present? Ross (1930, p. 29) argues that the action required in many situations is self-evident or obvious. Ross did not mean obvious in the sense of ingrained natural instinct but self-evident in a way that reasonable people would acknowledge the probability that a moral duty is present. For example, in scenario 1 in table 2–1, the distribution manager might inherently accept the argument that the duty of justice compels a more equitable distribution of products to the low income store, regardless of its other managerial complications.

How does a person handle situations where there is a conflict among duties? For example, in scenario 2 of table 2–1, the Chevy dealer's highly emotional, fear-laden advertising may violate the implicit duty of fidelity the dealers have with consumers to refrain from manipulative promotion. Conversely, if the crash test data are accurate, the dealers may feel that the duty of self-improvement justifies implementing the campaign. How can such conflicts be resolved? Ross is clear, if not completely satisfying, on this point:

> It may again be objected that . . . there are these various and often conflicting types of prima facie duty that leaves us with no principle upon which to discern what is our actual duty in particular circumstances. . . . For when we have to choose . . . the "ideal utilitarian" theory can only fall back on an opinion . . . that one of the two duties is more urgent. [1930, p. 23]

Thus, conflicts among duties are resolved by our opinion of how the general duties apply after we have carefully assessed the situation.

This discussion may lead one to conclude that the Ross (1930) framework is rather arbitrary and incomplete. Certainly these are valid criticisms. However, the Ross framework interjects several important insights critical to the practice of ethical marketing. First, the Ross theory encourages managers to determine what their prima facie duties might be and to discharge them unless other such obligations take precedence. Thus, if a marketer knowingly misrepresents product quality to buyers, a duty of fidelity has been violated;

if sales representatives are let go when their sales fall below quota, a duty of gratitude may be violated; and so on. Second, the Ross framework emphasizes the constant moral obligations that always exist. It deemphasizes the approach of attempting to predict results in morally sensitive situations. Such outcome-oriented approaches frequently are used to rationalize potentially unethical behavior. For instance (again alluding to the scenarios), if Jones Co. exports the subsugural-laden soft drinks, they may speculate that consumers will not be hurt because the test data are invalid; if Thrifty Supermarket continues its distribution policy, they may decide it is doubtful outsiders will ever know it. Thus, concern with outcomes may prohibit the examination of impending moral duties on the premise that no harm will probably occur.

The Proportionality Framework

Another multidimensional model of business ethics has been articulated by Garrett (1966). The framework is distinctive because it was specifically developed with the practicing business manager in mind. In addition, it attempts to combine the appealing utilitarian concern for outcomes ("the greatest good . . . ") with the Kantian preoccupation with process or means. Garrett contends that ethical decisions consist of three components: intention, means, and end.

Intention has to do with the motivation behind a person's actions. Garrett (1966) believes that what is intended by a particular act is an important component of morality. For example, the organization that formulates a code of marketing ethics motivated solely by the belief that such a code will help sell its products to religious or sectarian organizations has not acted ethically. Thus, purity of intention is a factor in evaluating the ethics of a specific situation.

Means refers to the process or method used to effect intention and bring about specific ends. For example, suppose a sales representative whose family has recently incurred some substantial medical expenses begins to overstock her customers and pad her expense account. The intention, to relieve the financial distress of her family, is good; however, the means chosen to accomplish this goal is unethical.

End deals with outcomes, results, or consequences of actions. Utilitarian theory is based on the precept that the correctness of an action is determined by calculating the end goodness that results from that action compared with the goodness produced by alternative actions that could have been taken. Garrett's (1966) view is that ends are properly evaluated by analyzing the intrinsic nature of the acts rather than the consequences produced by these acts. Or, put another way, it will not allow permitting the end to justify the means. For example, suppose a brewing company announces that all the revenues from beer sales at a new hotel will be donated to charity. However, suppose the distribution rights at the hotel had been obtained by bribery. In this instance, the ends (a charitable contribution) do not justify the means (bribery).

These three elements have been synthesized by Garrett into his *principle of proportionality:*

> I am responsible for whatever I will as a means or an end. If both the means and end I am willing are good, in and of themselves, I may ethically permit or risk the foreseen but unwilled side effects if, and only if, I have a proportionate reason for doing so. To put it another way: I am not responsible for unwilled side effects if I have sufficient reason for risking or permitting them, granted always that what I do will, as a means or an end, is good. [1966, p. 8]

This principle raises a number of issues that require clarification. Most important, what is the nature of the side effects that are permitted? Garrett (1966) elaborates on these issues with several amplifications.

> It is unethical to will, whether as a means or an end, a major evil to another. [p. 12]

By major evil, Garrett means the loss of a significant capacity that an entity (person or organization, for example) needs to function. For example, in scenario 3 (table 2–1) suppose the substance subsugural had been linked to birth defects when consumed by pregnant women. Jones Co.'s strategy of exporting the product to avoid writing off a major financial loss (the end goal) would not be ethical because consumption of the cola would have a reasonable probability of causing major evil: a significant birth defect in a newborn.

> It is unethical to risk or permit a major evil to another without a proportionate reason. [p. 14]

The concept of proportionate reason is at focus here. The principle of proportionality specifies that a proportionate reason exists when the good willed as means or end equals or outweighs the harmful side effects that are not willed as either a means or end. For example, again examine the scenario 3 situation. Suppose Jones Co. researchers knew for a fact that the government studies were invalid and that subsugural would soon be declared benign by the FDA. This would constitute a proportionate reason for going ahead with the soft drink export.

> It is unethical to will, risk or permit a minor evil without a proportionate reason. [p. 14]

By minor evil, Garrett means a harm to physical goods or to some means that are useful but not necessary for an entity's operation. For instance, in scenario 5 (table 2–1), suppose the potential reduction of quality in the Buy American TV sets is such that, even if it occurred, the video and audio difference in the TVs could not be perceived by consumers. In this case, the minor evil (an unstated quality difference) would be justified by a proportionate reason (higher market share for Buy American and lower prices for consumers).

It must be acknowledged that certain dimensions of the proportionality model remain vague or at least subjective. For example, where does one draw the line between a major evil and a minor evil? Attempting to influence a purchasing agent with a pair of $10 sports tickets (scenario 4) is probably a minor evil. However, if the company receives the contract because of the gift and the competing bidder goes bankrupt, does it become a major evil? Similarly, what constitutes a proportionate reason? In scenario 6, is it a proportionate reason for the financially ailing Smith and Smith agency to take the PR contract, knowing that a demur will simply result in another reputable agency's doing the work?

Despite these difficulties, the Garrett (1966) framework has much to recommend its use. Basically, it provides the marketing manager with a three-phase battery of questions that can be used to analyze the ethics of a given situation:

Phase 1: Given the situation, what is willed as a means and end? If a major evil is willed, the action is unethical and should not be taken.

Phase 2: Given the situation, what are the foreseen but unwilled side effects? If there is no proportionate reason for risking or allowing a major evil or willing a minor evil, the action is unethical and should not be taken.

Phase 3: Given the situation, what are the alternative actions? Is there an alternative to the end that would provide more good consequences and fewer evil consequences? Not to select this alternative would be unethical.

Notice that the three elements of any ethical decision—intent (will), means, and end—are incorporated into the framework. Moreover, the approach is consistent with the type of analysis many managers already conduct in their planning and forecasting efforts; that is, it involves attempting to predict outcomes of strategies and compare them with alternative options. This lends a dimension of familiarity to the model for planning-oriented managers. Finally, the principle of proportionality provides a flexible model of ethical decision making because it does not postulate specific trespasses. It provides general, universal guidelines that can be applied to a wide variety of managerial situations.

The Social Justice Framework

In intellectual circles, one of the most influential books on the subject of ethics has been John Rawls's A *Theory of Social Justice* (1971). Rawls, a Harvard University moral philosopher, proposed a detailed system of social ethics that attempted to maximize rewards to those most disadvantaged in a given social system. Rawls used deductive reasoning to arrive at his conception of social justice.

Central to Rawls's (1971) thesis is the construction of an imaginary state of affairs called the *original position*. This hypothetical situation would be somewhat analogous to the time frame *preceding* a game of chance. The participants do not know in advance what the game of chance might hold—that is, if they will be winners or losers. So, too, in the original position, people do not know what their place in society will be once the game of life begins; they do not know their social status, educational opportunities, class position, physical or intellectual abilities, and so on. They might be king or pauper.

Why is the original position and the so-called veil of ignorance it imposes so important? Rawls (1971) believes that hypothesizing such a state is the only way to reason to a pure system of justice—that is, one that is unblemished by the knowledge of the current state of affairs. For example, if a person knows that he has wealth in the society, that person will likely consider a system that heavily taxes the rich to provide for the poor as unjust. Or, if a person is poor, she will probably feel the opposite (p. 18–19). Therefore, what Rawls seeks to obtain from the original position is a vehicle that can be used to deduce an ideal system of justice—one that rational people would choose if they knew nothing of what their station in life might be.

Rawls's (1971) entire treatise is devoted to specifying the conclusions or consequences at which persons would arrive for assigning rights and duties in a social system, given the original position. Rawls's arguments defy easy explanation, but basically he concludes that rational people (not knowing what their fortune will be) would utilize a *minimax* method of decision making; that is, they would choose a system that minimizes the maximum loss they could incur. They would opt for a system that seeks to avoid harsh losses (for example, slavery, starvation, indigence) for those at the bottom of the scale, because conceivably this could be their position.

Rawls concludes (1971, p. 60) that we would arrive at two principles of justice, the *liberty principle* and the *difference principle:*

The liberty principle states that each person is to have an equal right to the most extensive basic liberty compatible with a similar liberty for others.

The difference principle states that social and economic inequalities are to be arranged so that they are both to the greatest benefit of the least disadvantaged and attached to positions and offices open to all.

These principles require some elaboration. The liberty principle guarantees equal opportunity as well as basic liberties such as the freedom of speech, the right to vote, the right to due process of the law, and ownership of property. In addition, the principle explicitly states that greater liberty should always be preferred to lesser liberty provided it can be attained without major social dysfunctions. For example, suppose a law specified that airline pilots should be between 40 and 60 years of age, but data showed that this job could be done with the proper training by anyone between 25 and 70; it would be a violation of the principle of liberty to accept the more restricted scheme. Holding that airline pilots must be between 40 and 60 would be unethical to those outside this age bracket who could perform the job. Similarly, an industry code that mandated that all bicycles should be built to withstand crashes with automobiles up to 55 MPH would also likely violate the principle.

The difference principle specifies the conditions that must exist to act contrary to the liberty principle. In essence, inequality of economic goods or social position (that is, the lessening of liberty) can only be tolerated when the practice that generates the inequality works to the advantage of every individual affected or to the advantage of those members of the system who are least well off. However, the basic liberties like the right to vote can never be traded for economic goods or temporary social position. In this fashion, Rawls's (1971) system is a bold contrast to that of classical utilitarianism. Why? Utilitarians would permit some individuals to become worse off as long as a greater number of others become better off. The Rawls framework claims to prohibit the disadvantaged becoming more so. It is highly egalitarian in the sense that actions are never permitted that disadvantage the least well off; the tendency instead is a "drive to equality" (pp. 100–108) that over time should benefit those worse off in a particular system more than those better off.

What are the ramifications of the social justice theory on marketing ethics? In all fairness, it should be emphasized that Rawls (1971) did not conceive his theory would be readily transferred to marketing or, for that matter, business ethics. However, the two guiding principles alone seem to suggest some enormous implications. The principle of liberty emphasizes the inherent right of individual persons to determine their destiny and always to be treated equitably by others. This maximization of personal liberty, subject to the claims of others, would seem to underscore the consumer's right to safety, information, choice, and redress. Applied to a specific situation (for example, scenario 5 in table 2–1), the liberty principle would seem to demand that Buy American Electronics Co. inform consumers of the change in components and the possible reduction in quality of the second generation System X sets. Not to take this course of action would unfairly restrict the liberty of choice consumers have in this situation.

The difference principle holds an even more striking implication. It emphasizes the fact that it would be unethical to exploit one group for the benefit of others. A particularly severe violation of the principle would occur if a group that was relatively worse off were victimized to benefit a better situated group. For example, in scenario 6 of table 2–1, the difference principle would probably suggest that the Smith and Smith Agency forego the PR contract because its acceptance could add legitimacy to the ruling foreign government and further jeopardize the position of a worse off group—namely, the citizens of the totalitarian country. On a more general plane, Rawls's principles would seem to affirm the ethical validity of the marketing concept that formally incorporates the rights of a less powerful group (consumers) into the planning and goal setting of a more powerful group (business).

The Value of the Frameworks

The potential contribution of these frameworks should be clearly stated. First, the purpose of these perspectives is not to provide precise answers to ethical dilemmas. In fact, an attempt to apply more than one framework to a particular situation could lead to a conflicting conclusion. For example, in scenario 1 of table 2–1, the Rawlsian would undoubtedly conclude that Thrifty Supermarkets must cease and desist its practice of sending its lower quality products to the economically inefficient retail store because this allocation scheme further discriminates against the already disadvantaged, low income shopper. In contrast, one could argue, using Ross's duty of gratitude as a rationale, that Thrifty Supermarkets owes its loyal, upscale customers a special status when it comes to the selection of their meats and produce.

If these frameworks do not answer tough questions dealing with marketing ethics, what is their value? Their major purpose is to be used as a pedagogical tool to sensitize managers to the factors that are important in coming to grips with ethical issues. There are few irrefutably right answers to these questions, but the fact that management has systematically considered the options along with their ethical ramifications is of ultimate importance. Thus, the contribution of such devices is to provide marketing managers with a philosophical mnemonic that serves to remind them of their ethical responsibilities. The perspectives provided by writers such as Ross, Garrett, and Rawls emphasize that the factors involved in reaching an ethical judgment are deeper than the jingoism of ethical maxims such as "Thou shalt be good."

Toward a Theory of Marketing Ethics

As noted earlier, there is nothing supernatural about these frameworks. Their adoption will not automatically generate ethical behavior in marketing; these models do not explain or predict the incidence of unethical behavior that can occur in marketing. However, taken together, they introduce certain advantages to marketing educators, practitioners, and researchers.

For educators, the frameworks provide perspectives that go beyond the proverbial ethical maxim. The frameworks represent quasi-models of intermediate sophistication that suggest a rationale for why particular moral choices might be made. In this sense, the introduction of this material establishes a useful background for the classroom analysis of marketing cases having ethical implications. Explaining the models to students provides the educator with the opportunity to inject ethical considerations into the discussion of mainstream marketing strategy.

For practitioners, the frameworks suggest a list of possible factors that might be utilized to decide tough-question situations regarding ethics. Some speculation about the possible application of these frameworks to real world situations was discussed earlier. If the answer to any of the following questions is yes, then action A is most probably unethical and should be reconsidered; if every question truly can be answered with no, then action A is probably ethical. Consider the following possible sequence:

Does action A violate the law?

Does action A violate any of the following moral obligations:
   Duties of fidelity?
   Duties of gratitude?
   Duties of justice?
   Duties of beneficence?
   Duties of self-improvement?
   Duties of nonmaleficence?

Does action A violate any special obligations stemming from the type of marketing organization in question (for example, the special duty of pharmaceutical firms to provide safe products)?

Is the intent of action A evil?

Are any major evils likely to result from or because of action A?

Is a satisfactory alternative B, which produces equal or more good with less evil than A, being knowingly rejected?

Does action A infringe upon the inalienable liberties of the consumer?

Does action A leave another person or group less well off? Is this person or group already relatively underprivileged?

The questions need not be pursued in any lockstep fashion but can be discussed in an order dictated by the situation.

For researchers, the frameworks may suggest some of the components necessary for the construction of a model describing ethical behavior in marketing. To be sure, such a model should specify appropriate standards of ethical action; demarcate the factors, both internal and external, that influence the likelihood of ethical behavior; and provide a listing of the organizational variables that might be adjusted to enhance the probability of ethical action. In this vein, the Ross (1930) framework identifies some fundamental duties or obligations that are incumbent upon managers and thereby could constitute potential ethical standards. The Garrett (1966) framework specifies three variables—intention, process (or means), and outcomes—that the researcher would have to analyze to have a relatively accurate picture of the ethics inherent in a particular action. It may very well be that different internal and external variables influence different dimensions of the ethical action. For example, the attitude of top management (an internal factor) may be a major influence on the process or means a manager selects to handle an ethical question; in contrast, professional standards (an external variable) may be a major determinant of a manager's intent in a given situation. Thus, Garrett provides insight into the necessary requisites for empirically measuring the ethics of a given action. Finally, the Rawls (1971) framework suggests some special considerations that could be introduced into an ethical evaluation; namely, he provides a justification for giving special ethical consideration to parties that are relatively worse off (that is, socially disadvantaged). Rawls, in effect, sketches the moral equivalent of affirmative action ethics for marketing managers.

Assuming the frameworks of Ross, Garrett, and Rawls could be integrated into one grand theory, it is still doubtful that the theory would constitute a satisfactory model of marketing ethics. Nevertheless, given the relevance of ethical questions in marketing, it is important that marketing academics continue to strive to develop a theory of marketing ethics.

On a pragmatic level, the frameworks stimulate several suggestions concerning marketing ethics that could have a beneficial influence at the macro level. First, Garrett's concern with major and minor evils suggests that researchers should attempt to rank in terms of severity the various ethical abuses that regularly occur in the field of marketing. Since it is naive to believe that significant unethical conduct in marketing can be eliminated overnight, the resulting ranking could constitute a makeshift "hit list" that would then single out particular areas for concern and remedial action. For example, the passage of the Foreign Corrupt Practices Act (1977) forced most corporations operating overseas to re-examine the propriety of their selling practices. In publicizing areas of acute ethical concern, the hope is that the marketing discipline could short circuit the necessity of legislation to engender ethical reform.

Second, Ross's compilation of prima facie duties, a listing formulated at the most general level, should motivate textbook writers in marketing to propose a listing of what they consider to be the minimum ethical responsibilities incumbent on practicing marketing managers. While such specifications will undoubtedly cause some controversy and debate, the subsequent sifting and winnowing will spotlight the topic of ethics and, we hope, raise the moral sensitivites of students.

Third, Rawls's concern with the multifaceted impact of business policies on various groups in society (especially the most disadvantaged) should ideally stimulate case writers to incorporate ethical problems and analysis into the cases they author. The reason for this is that the case method is the best pedagogical tool for getting the student to visualize the influence of an organizational decision on sundry stakeholders. Surely an inference that can be drawn from Rawls is that it is the duty of every discipline (including marketing) to foster mechanisms that will generate ethical introspection. The reputation of marketers may depend on it.

References

Alderson, Wroe. 1964. "Ethics, Ideologies and Sanctions." In *Report of the Committee on Ethical Standards and Professional Practices*. Chicago: American Marketing Association.

Bartels, Robert. 1967. "A Model for Ethics in Marketing." *Journal of Marketing* 31 (January), pp. 20–26.

Beauchamp, Tom L., and Norman E. Bowie. 1979. *Ethical Theory and Business*. Englewood Cliffs, N.J.: Prentice-Hall, Inc., pp. 11–14.

Colihan, William J., Jr. 1967. "Ethics in Today's Marketing." In *Changing Marketing Systems*, Reed Moyers, ed. Chicago: American Marketing Association, pp. 164–166.

Farmer, Richard N. 1967. "Would You Want Your Daughter to Marry a Marketing Man?" *Journal of Marketing* 31 (January), pp. 1–3.

———. 1977. "Would You Want Your Son to Marry a Marketing Lady?" *Journal of Marketing* 41 (January), pp. 15–18.

Ferrell, O.C., and K. Mark Weaver. 1978. "Ethical Beliefs of Marketing Managers," *Journal of Marketing* 42 (July), pp. 69–73.

Fisk, George. 1982. "Contributor's Guide for Choice of Topics for Papers," *Journal of Macromarketing* 2 (Spring), pp. 5–6.

Garrett, Thomas. 1966. *Business Ethics*. Englewood Cliffs, N.J.: Prentice-Hall, Inc.

Hunt, Shelby D. 1976. *Marketing Theory: Conceptual Foundations of Research in Marketing*. Columbus, Ohio: Grid, Inc.

Kelley, Eugene J. 1969. "Ethical Considerations for a Scientifically Oriented Marketing Management." In *Science in Marketing Management*, M.S. Mayer, ed. Toronto, Ontario: York University, pp. 69–87.

Kizilbash, A.H., et al. 1979. "Social Auditing for Marketing Managers." *Industrial Marketing Management* 8, pp. 1–6.

McMahon, Thomas V. 1967. "A Look at Marketing Ethics." *Atlanta Economic Review* 17 (March).

Murphy, Patrick E., and Gene R. Laczniak. 1981. "Marketing Ethics: A Review with Implications for Managers, Educators and Researchers." In *Review of Marketing 1981*, B. Enis and K. Roering, eds. Chicago: American Marketing Association, pp. 251–266.

Murphy, Patrick E., Gene R. Laczniak, and Robert F. Lusch. 1978. "Ethical Guidelines for Business and Social Marketing." *Journal of the Academy of Marketing Science* 6 (Summer), pp. 197–205.

Patterson, James M. 1966. "What Are the Social and Ethical Responsibilities of Marketing Executives?" *Journal of Marketing* 30 (July), pp. 12–15.

Pruden, Henry. 1971. "Which Ethics for Marketers?" In *Marketing and Social Issues*, John R. Wish and Stephen H. Gamble, eds. New York: John Wiley & Sons, pp. 98–104.

Rawls, John. 1971. *A Theory of Justice*. Cambridge, Mass.: Harvard University Press.

Robin, Donald P. 1980. "Value Issues in Marketing." In *Theoretical Developments in Marketing*, C.W. Lamb and P.M. Dunne, eds. Chicago: American Marketing Association, pp. 142–145.

Ross, William David. 1930. *The Right and the Good*. Oxford: Clarendon Press.

Rudelius, William, and Rogene A. Buchholz. 1979. "Ethical Problems of Purchasing Managers." *Harvard Business Review* (March–April), pp. 8, 12, and 14.

Sartorius, Rolf E. 1975. *Individual Conduct and Social Norms: A Utilitarian Account of Social Union and Rule of Law*. Belmont, Calif.: Dickenson Publishing.

Singer, Peter. 1976. "Freedoms and Utility in the Distribution of Health Care." In *Ethics and Health Policy*, R. Veatch and R. Branson, eds. Cambridge, Mass.: Ballinger Publishing.

Steiner, John F. 1976. "The Prospect of Ethical Advisors for Business Corporation." *Business and Society* (Spring), pp. 5–10.

Sturdivant, Frederick D., and A. Benton Cocanougher. 1973. "What Are Ethical Marketing Practices?" *Harvard Business Review* 51 (November-December), pp. 10–12.

Walton, Clarence C. 1961. "Ethical Theory, Societal Expectations and Marketing Practices." In *The Social Responsibilities of Marketing*, William D. Stevens, ed. Chicago: American Marketing Association, pp. 8–24.

Westing, J. Howard. 1967. "Some Thoughts on the Nature of Ethics in Marketing." In *Changing Marketing Systems*, Reed Moyer, ed. Chicago: American Marketing Association, pp. 161–163.

3
Implementing and Monitoring Ethics in Advertising

O.C. Ferrell

I n the late 1970s, Maidenform started the advertising appeal, "The Maidenform woman. You never know where she'll turn up." The advertisements feature a scantily clad model (figure 3–1) standing around fully clothed men. Women Against Pornography have given Maidenform a ZAP award for sexist advertising. The company maintains that the only way their merchandise can be properly shown is to put it on models. This advertising campaign creates an ethical dilemma for the company and interested members of society.

When advertisers operate according to accepted principles of right and wrong, they make proper ethical decisions. The question is what constitutes right and wrong. As discussed in Laczniak (1983b) and others, an action could be judged based on an examination of, for example, (1) theory of justice (protect the interest of all involved); (2) utilitarianism (greatest possible balance of value for all persons involved); or (3) a theory of rights (which specifies minimum levels of satisfaction along with standards that are independent of outcomes).

Today, ethical *relativism* is more popular in making ethical decisions about advertising than ethical *absolutism*, which assumes one true moral code. The middle ground of ethical relativism recognizes that while there may be different value systems, analysis of moral consequences and the establishment of limited moral principles are extremely important (Robin 1980). The Maidenform ethical dilemma is a good example of a decision that is in the middle ground of ethical relativism. One party sees the use of live models in advertisements as the logical way to promote lingerie, while another group perceives such provocative photos as exploitive.

Ethical relativism is illustrated by Laczniak's (1983a) fourteen propositions to enable management to deal with the subject of business ethics. The various propositions offered range from alternative standards of ethical practice (for example, the golden rule) to prescriptive propositions calling for codes of ethics. The advertising industry probably contains a distinctive ethic of its own in addition to the ethical standards of the surrounding cultural and social environment. To apply absolute, "thou shalt not knowingly do harm,"

Figure 3–1. Advertisement Illustrating an Ethical Dilemma in What Can Be Presented Tastefully in Advertising

types of moral rules without exploring the purpose and scope of advertising in the larger social and economic system would be a mistake. For many advertising decision makers, ethical behavior is directly related to their ability to meet performance objectives.

Most discussions of ethics in advertising in the press and trade publications focus on the legality of advertising practice and the existence and enforcement of industrywide codes of ethics. General platitudes about the necessity of ethical advertising or professional conduct are found in most companies and ad agencies. The National Advertising Review Board (NARB) (supported by the National Council of Better Business Bureaus) screens national advertisements to check for honesty and processes complaints about deceptive advertising. For example, the NARB claimed that Fram misled consumers by implying that regular and frequent changes of their oil filter would save large repair bills. According to the NARB the ad used exaggeration and so-called puff techniques with claims that are subject to qualitative and quantitive measurement.

Three questions seem most important in analyzing ethics with respect to the practice of advertising. Is advertising by its very nature intrinsically or frequently unethical? How do organizational dynamics influence ethics-related decisions in advertising? What should be done to maintain and, if necessary, improve ethical conduct in advertising? This chapter addresses these issues by synthesizing theoretical and empirical research related to implementing and monitoring ethics in advertising.

Impact on Consumer Autonomy

Consider the following ads and the questions they raise that illustrate ethical issues in advertising:

> *Ad description:* The National Rifle Association (NRA) has featured an eight-year-old boy holding a BB gun in one of its ads. The copy discussed the boy's fondness for his gun and that his father taught him how to use it responsibly. Reasons for the boy's joining the NRA were also included.

> *Ethical questions:* Are BB guns safe for eight-year-old children? Are children capable of understanding the danger and risks involved in using guns? Is the NRA an appropriate group for an eight-year-old to join?

> *Ad description:* Chivas Regal brand of scotch promoted their product by the line "What the rich give the wealthy." This social status appeal shows a china decanter with a velvet sack for about $50 per bottle price in the ad.

Ethical questions: Is this product what the rich really give the wealthy? Has this statement been quantified or substantiated? Is it possible that people of modest income most typically buy this product?

Ad description: Virginia Slims cigarettes has long used the slogan, "You've come a long way, baby." A recent ad depicts a young modern day woman dressed in camping attire and shows three photos in the background of women from an earlier era doing laundry on a washboard and other outdoor chores. The ad contains a caption under these photos that states, "Virginia Slims remembers the many pleasures of a woman's day while camping in the great outdoors."

Ethical questions: Is this product dangerous to your health? What does camping have to do with cigarettes? Is the description of the pleasures associated with camping misleading?

Taken together, do these advertisements manipulate human hopes and desires as well as result in undesirable purchasing? Do these advertisements help to control the behavior of consumers? Levitt (1970) has stated that "embellishment and distortion are among advertising's legitimate and socially desirable purposes." To reject these techniques of advertising would be "to deny man's honest needs and values." Based on Levitt's statement, would all four of these advertising and promotion examples contribute to "honest needs and values?" Or are these examples of embellishment and distortion directed at behavior control through puffery, manipulation, and deception?

While the ethics of the ads described here are debatable, figure 3–2, which shows the case of M&M's "now even bigger pack," is a clearly defined misrepresentation. However, the following explanation (via personal correspondence) by a Mars regional president seems to indicate the M&M's misrepresentation was not intentional:

> We can see how a consumer would be confused by finding two packs of our product in the marketplace with the same expiration date but different weights, and the lower weight pack reading "Now Even Bigger Pack." We regret that this incident occurred. However, we assure you that nothing deceptive or misleading was intended by our packaging. In fact, it was an example of our company increasing the value of its products.
>
> In March 1982, M&M/MARS increased the portion size of all single bars and packs without raising the products' prices. For "M&M's" Plain Chocolate Candies, the weight increased 10.4% from 1.44 ozs. to 1.59 ozs. The packages read "Now Even Bigger Pack."
>
> Because consumer response to the bigger pack was so favorable, we again increased the weight of "M&M's" Plain Chocolate Candies. In September, we began packaging in their new weight—1.69 ozs.
>
> The explanation for the same expiration date is as follows. We mark all products made in a one-month period with the same expiration date. During August we labeled "M&M's" Plain Chocolate Candies with July '83 expira-

Less of the product, but an even 'bigger pack'

To the Editor: Mars Inc. has provided us with an excellent example of product misrepresentation.

Their regular-size pack of M&Ms weighs in at 1.69 ozs. or 48.1 grams, is a single serving, has 240 calories and is marked good until July '83.

Their new package (marked brightly: "Now even bigger pack") weighs in at 1.59 ozs. or 45.1 grams, is a single serving, has only 220 calories and is also good until July '83.

Believe it or not, I found both packs facing me in the same vending machine.

Randy S. Gillett,
Evanston, Ill.

Figure 3–2. Apparent Product Misrepresentation in Packaging and Promotion of M&M's Candies

tions. The switch to larger packages occurred at the same time. This then explains why two different packages bore the same expiration date.

Both weight increases of "M&M's" Plain Chocolate Candies were implemented without any increase in our wholesale price. We will continue our commitment to provide customers with quality and value.

Again, thank you for bringing this matter to our attention. We are currently reviewing production processes so that an incident such as this does not occur again.

In contrast, the NRA ad involves a debate on the ethics of NRA objectives and children's advertising ethics; that is, do children need special protection? The Chivas ad might be defended based on Levitt's (1970) view that advertising increases the perceived value of the product. The product advertised as exclusive provides the desired images or symbols that some consumers seek. However, the Virginia Slims ad is questionable for several reasons. This product has been identified by medical authorities as dangerous to one's health. Is there an attempt to create misleading product attributes? Is a product that is dangerous unfairly associated with the desire for personal fulfillment?

To answer questions like these, Arrington (1982), a philosophy professor, examined advertising to determine if techniques were being used "to manipulate and control the behavior of consumers and violate their autonomy." Arrington uses four concepts:

Autonomous desire: Does advertising create desires that are not truly our own? He answers that, in most cases, autonomy is not violated. This is proposed because there are usually repeat purchases of controversial items like cigarettes without regret or remorse.

Rational desire and choice: Does advertising lead us to act on irrational desires or to make irrational choices? In rejoinder, he argues we often wish to purchase psychological benefits that provide subjective satisfaction.

Free choice: Is advertising so strong that we could not resist an appeal? He reasons that most of our purchase decisions are in fact free choice because we purchase for a reason.

Control of manipulation: Under what conditions does manipulation occur? He concludes that the advertiser influences more than controls an audience. Most often, advertising intends to induce a desire for a particular product, given that the purchaser already has the basic desire.

Applying the concepts to the case of advertising, Arrington argues that advertising cannot be found guilty of intrinsically or frequently violating the consumers' autonomy in any of the relevant senses of this notion (1982, p. 3). He concludes that advertising may, but does not frequently, control behavior, produce compulsive behavior, or create wants that are not rational.

After discussing the philosophical dimensions of the value of advertising, most supporters of a free enterprise economy like Arrington (1982) would come down on the side of advertisers. Advertising is not intrinsically unethical based on evaluations by Arrington or on an examination of the theories of justice, utilitarianism, or rights. Therefore, the motives of those who create the purpose and content of advertising are a key concern in judging action.

All definitions of unethical advertising are value judgments. Blatantly unethical advertising is rare. Puffery, mildly suggestive claims, and claims to provide fulfillment of hidden needs are usually viewed as acceptable in our society. Claims designed purposely to mislead or deceive the consumer may be judged unethical by moral philosophy but could be viewed as ethical by utilitarianism. For example, an antismoking advertisement by the American Heart Association could be viewed by some as having good consequences even if it made a false claim about cigarettes that effectively discourages smoking. Consider the American Heart Association's antismoking advertisement in figure 3–3 that parodies the Virginia Slims well-known line. Should questionable advertising be countered with advertisements like this? Arguments can be advancd on both sides of the issue. In summary, any suggestions for improving the ethical conduct of advertisers should recognize that it is impossible to reach an agreement on what criteria to use in defining unethical advertising.

A Review of Advertising Ethics

To understand better the ethics in advertising issue, it is helpful to examine some of the history that underlies the morality of advertising issues. Murphy and Laczniak (1981) provided the following useful summary.

The ethics of advertising, like sales, has come under question almost continuously (Packard 1957; Galbraith 1958). Because advertising is such a visible element of marketing, this situation is not surprising. Furthermore, ethical issues come up with respect to the role of advertising agencies' dealing with their clients as well as the advertiser-consumer linkage.

A thorough discussion of advertising ethics is contained in Wright and Mertes's (1974) readings book. In this work, selections about advertising ethics were written by Alderson, who discussed the reconciliation of Christian ethics with the U.S. economy; Levitt (1970); and a variety of scholars from outside the field of marketing who used their fields of religion, philosophy, and history to comment on advertising ethics. Despite the appearance of an advertising code of ethics in the 1920s, the various authors chronicle many continuing abuses, including puffery and exaggerated claims. Several prescriptions for raising the level of ethics in advertising were presented by these writers, including Levitt's (1970) classic defense of advertising ethics. In that article, Levitt admitted that advertisers typically tried to persuade and manipulate consumers but that these efforts were not fundamentally different or as controversial as the efforts of artists, politicians, and editorial writers to manipulate ideas in the minds of citizens.

At the 1971 American Marketing Association (AMA) Educators' Conference, Boulding (1971) gave a speech on the ethics of persuasion. He listed four major ethical criticisms of the persuasion industry:

Figure 3–3. Parody of Cigarette Ad which Discourages Smoking

1. The contention that persuasion of an individual violates the person's inherent rights;
2. The fact that the persuasion industry leads to certain human addictions;
3. Simple dishonesty—that is, persuaders are only trying to make money but not propagate the truth;
4. The idea that persuasion frequently degenerates into vulgarization.

Boulding's thoughtful analysis concludes with a call for a continuing search by marketers for answers to tough ethical questions in advertising.

Several new topics have surfaced in the area of advertising ethics. Consoli (1976) advocated that advertisers display a high standard of ethics in using comparative advertising. Also, the stereotyping of women in advertising was mentioned as another ethical issue in this article. Turk (1979) examined what he labeled as the "ethical morass" of advertising to children. He felt both government and industry are caught in this trap. He argues that marketers and broadcasters feign concern for children's health but also want to perpetuate highly profitable television programs aimed at children. At the same time, Turk likened Federal Trade Commission (FTC) staff to moral crusaders of another era and states that their proposals are too severe for acceptance. Krugman and Ferrell (1981) investigated the ethical perceptions held by advertising practitioners, ad agency account managers, and corporate ad managers regarding their peers in the organization and others with whom they interact. It is not surprising that they found that respondents believe they possess higher ethical standards than their peers. The authors concluded that favorable ethical performance should be rewarded and widely disseminated and that top management should use their perceived higher ethical standards to influence the members of the firm.

Recently, the popular press has taken notice of current advertising campaigns that make extensive use of sex appeal. Bronson (1980) examined several campaigns and discussed the role of the network censor in deciding which ads are not in good taste. The use of sex appeal is especially prevalent in promoting designer jeans (Frons 1980; Bronson and Birnhaum 1980). The use of models clad provocatively in jeans and the use of suggestive language in television commercials are commonplace in this type of advertising. One writer captured the flavor of these campaigns: "Almost all TV ads for designer jeans exploit fantasy in campaigns that seem to stretch the tenets of truth in advertising" (Frons 1980, p. 85).

One thing seems certain: The overt nature of advertising lays it open to questions of an ethical nature. This point was noted by Greyser and Reece (1971) when introducing their classic survey of businesspeople's attitudes toward advertising: "Perhaps because it touches the public in so many ways and throughout the day, advertising seems to be receiving a constant barrage of criticism from both activists and the public."

After concentrating on the business perspective toward advertising, Greyser and Reece (1971) concluded that subscribers to a leading business publication were increasingly uneasy about the truthfulness and ultimate social impact of advertising. Krugman and Ferrell (1981) reached the conclusion that advertisers clearly distinguished between the acceptability of certain practices. Ethics are seen to be a matter of degree rather than either absolutely wrong or absolutely right. Issues of a more overt nature that need more than tacit approval are judged to be more unethical than issues that are more covert and easily rationalized. For example, padding an expense account more than 10 percent or manipulating a situation to make a superior or subordinate look bad are seen as highly unethical, while not reporting the violations of others and taking extra personal time are seen as more acceptable behavior. In sum, the less overt and more easily rationalized behaviors are believed to be more acceptable and more widely practiced.

Surveys of marketing managers indicate that knowing what is right or wrong in an organization is often difficult. Also, findings from a survey of practicing marketing managers (Ferrell and Weaver 1978) indicate that respondents believed they are more ethical than the ethical codes of conduct in their organization.

Moreover, marketers surveyed felt that they were more ethical than their peers, top management, or the organization. But, additional analysis of the data (Zey-Ferrell, Weaver, and Ferrell 1979) indicate that respondents tend to adopt the ethical behavior of their peers or top management regardless of their personal beliefs. Thus, individual members of the respondent's organization were most influential in determining the respondents' reported ethical behavior. The practitioners indicated that they went along with the group rather than sticking to their own ethical standards. This situation could create both personal and organizational ethical crises.

Figure 3–4 illustrates a framework for understanding the ethical/unethical behavior in advertising organizations. An implication of this model is that ethical and unethical behaviors are influenced by the opportunity to engage in questionable practices and by the process of interacting with people who are a part of the organizational context.

Suggestions for Improved Ethical Conduct

Based on the research findings and philosophical concepts discussed in this chapter, advertisers should ask the following questions:

1. Are my peers ethically sound? Do I follow their behavior even if they are wrong or possibly engage in illegal behavior?

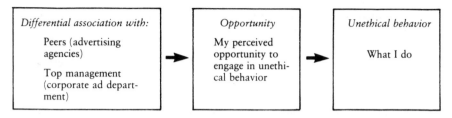

Figure 3–4. The Two-Stage Model of Ethical/Unethical Behavior in Advertising Agencies and Corporate Advertising Departments

2. Do I point out behaviors that are potentially unethical and damaging to myself and the welfare of the firm?
3. Have I developed my personal values and ethical standards based on a philosophy that is consistent with my culture and society?
4. How should I react to codes of ethics and ethical policies in my organization?
5. Are there industrywide professional standards or codes of ethics that should guide my decisions?

Although it is a personal decision, it is suggested here that advertisers should think about what is right or wrong and develop personal standards and stick to them. Depending solely on the decisions of peers or top management to guide ethical decisions has resulted in disaster—for example, Watergate. Furthermore, research indicates that firms should reduce the opportunity for unethical behavior and develop ethics-related policies. The existence and enforcement of ethics-related policies has been shown to improve the ethical belief and behavior of employees. Based on a survey of marketing managers, Weaver and Ferrell conclude:

> A basic building block of the organizationl environment is corporate policy. Formal policy is an explicit statement to encourage beliefs and behaviors either ethical or unethical. Based on these findings, policy appears to . . . influence ethical conduct. If the associations discovered in this limited study are typical, individuals that make policy decisions must assume some part of the responsibility for the ethical environment of the organization. Also, these findings question the impact of codes of ethics that are not enforced; top management should establish policy as well as express a commitment to ethical conduct. [1977, p. 480]

It is easier to suggest policies on ethics than to develop codes to guide managers. A firm must use a systematic approach in assessing its environment and the value systems that will influence value judgments about its behavior. Consider part of the worldwide business conduct code developed by Caterpillar (1974) to guide its managers in making decisions:

1. Caterpillar employees shall not accept costly entertainment or gifts (except mementos and novelties of nominal value) from dealers, suppliers, and others with whom we do business.

2. Company employees are also required to make good faith efforts to avoid payment of gratuities or "tips" to certain public officials, even where such practices are customary. Where these payments are, as a practical matter, unavoidable, they must be limited to customary amounts; and may be made only to facilitate correct performance of the officials' duties.

If policies like these are developed and enforced through top management, the best opportunity exists for improved ethical conduct in advertising. As discussed earlier, however, any approach to improve ethical conduct in advertising will be debatable, but the failure to develop and enforce specific policies on ethical conduct in developing advertising will result in limited control over the effectiveness of advertising. Only with tight control over the total advertising process can unethical or questionable actions be avoided that could destroy the impact of advertising and provide negative consequences for society.

How does management develop appropriate ethics-related policies? Here are some issues on which to focus:

Evaluate the current situation

Are objectives stated in qualitative as well as quantitative terms?

Does the firm now have policies that can aid managers in solving ethical problems?

Does the firm receive information that can help in detecting ethical concerns and issues?

Does the firm have a mechanism for developing policies on ethics?

Assess the future

Are there ethical issues that could affect the firm's overall long-run performance?

Will management be willing to sanction those who violate the ethics-related policies?

Can management tolerate ethical decisions that result in lost sales, higher costs, and/or lower profits?

What top management believes (corporate advertising environments) and what peers do (advertising agency environments) are the best predictors of how a marketer will solve an ethical problem. Evaluating advertising based on profit relationships and not by qualitative criteria (including ethical principle) creates a situation that could accelerate distrust of the firm and advertising in general. To improve advertising, it is necessary to understand the intraorganizational environment and then to influence top management and peers (possibly by eliminating opportunity) to act ethically.

Conclusion

This chapter answers three questions about implementing and monitoring ethics in advertising. First, is advertising by its very nature intrinsically or frequently unethical? Based on Arrington's (1982) logical testing of advertising, we conclude that in general advertising by its nature and scope is not unethical. Advertising is best judged by examining its purpose and role in our economic system or society. A Marxist philosophy of society might dispute this view and position advertising as foreign to the true nature of the individual. Certainly, some advertisers use practices that most of the advertising industry and society would judge as unethical.

The next question addressed relates to how organizational dynamics have an impact on ethics-related decisions in advertising. Our conclusion is that unethical behavior is influenced by opportunity and the process of interacting with people who are a part of the organizational context. Peers or top management influence most ethical decisions related to advertising.

Finally, several suggestions were made for improving ethical conduct in advertising. Ethical decision making is conceptually complex, and a multiplicity of factors may influence the final outcome. To implement and monitor ethical decision making in advertising, all dimensions of ethics should be examined. It is important for advertisers to recognize that ethics has both philosophical and organizational dimensions. A manager must understand the environment and process of ethical decision making in advertising as well as embrace an ethical value system.

References

Arrington, Robert L. 1982. "Advertising and Behavior Control." *Journal of Business Ethics* 1 (February), p. 3.

Boulding, Kenneth. 1971. "The Ethics of Persuasion." Paper presented by AMA Educators' Conference, Minneapolis, August 30.

Bronson, Gail. 1980. "Sexual Pitches in Ads Become More Explicit and More Pervasive." *The Wall Street Journal*, (November 18), 1t.

———, and T. Birnbaum. 1980. "Some People Believe that Blue Jean Ads Are a Little Too Blue." *The Wall Street Journal*, October 7, p. 1.

Consoli, John. 1976. "Comparative Print Ads More Credible: Kershaw." *Editor and Publisher*, May 22, pp. 14 and 16.

Ferrell, O.C., and K. Mark Weaver. 1978. "Ethical Beliefs of Marketing Managers." Journal of Marketing 42 (July), pp. 69–73.

Ferrell, O.C., Mary Zey-Ferrell, and Dean Krugman. 1983. "Intraorganizational Influences on Ethical/Unethical Behavior among Corporate Clients and Advertising Agencies." *Journal of Macromarketing* (Spring), pp. 21–27.

Frons, Marc. 1980. "The Jeaning of America." *Newsweek,* October 6, pp. 83 and 85.

Galbraith, John Kenneth. 1958. *The Affluent Society.* Boston: Houghton Mifflin.

Greyser, Steven A., and Bonnie Reece. 1971. "Businessmen Look Hard at Advertising," *Harvard Business Review* 50 (May–June), pp. 18ff.

Krugman, Dean, and O.C. Ferrell. 1981. "The Organizational Ethics of Advertising: Corporate and Agency Views." *Journal of Advertising* 10 (Spring), p. 30.

Laczniak, G.R. 1983a. "Business Ethics: A Managers' Primer." *Business* (January-February-March), pp. 23–29.

——— . 1983b. "Framework for Analyzing Marketing Ethics." *Journal of Macromarketing* (Spring), pp. 7–18.

Levitt, Theodore. 1970. "The Morality (?) of Advertising." *Harvard Business Review* 48 (July–August), pp. 84–92.

Murphy, Patrick E., and Gene R. Laczniak. 1981. "Marketing Ethics: A Review with Implications for Managers, Educators and Researchers." In *Review of Marketing 1981,* B. Enis and K. Roering, eds. Chicago: American Marketing Association, pp. 251–266.

Packard, Vance. 1957. *The Hidden Persuaders.* New York: Pocket Books.

Robin, Donald P. 1980. "Value Issues in Marketing." In *Theoretical Developments in Marketing,* Charles W. Lamb, Jr., and Patrick M. Dunne, eds. Chicago: American Marketing Association Proceedings, p. 142

Turk, Peter. 1979. "Children's Television Advertising: An Ethical Morass for Business and Government." *Journal of Advertising* 8 (Winter), pp. 4–8.

Weaver, K. Mark, and O.C. Ferrell. 1977. "The Impact of Corporate Policy on Reported Ethical Beliefs and Behavior of Marketing Practitioners." In *Contemporary Marketing Thought,* Barnett Greenberg and Danny N. Bellenger, eds. Chicago: American Marketing Association Proceedings, pp. 477–481.

Wright, John S., and John E. Mertes, eds. 1974. *Advertising's Role in Society.* St. Paul: West Publishing, pp. 252–300.

Zey-Ferrell, Mary, K. Mark Weaver, and O.C. Ferrell. 1979. "Predicting Unethical Behavior among Marketing Practitioners. *Human Relations* 32 (June-July), pp. 557–561.

4

Studying Field Salespeople's Ethical Problems: An Approach for Designing Company Policies

Alan J. Dubinsky

Scenario 1. A young computer salesperson faced the following dilemma. A newly installed computer system continually malfunctioned. The customer demanded that the system be replaced with a new, not used, model. Unbeknown to the customer, management would replace the computer in need of repair with only a used model that looked new. The salesperson was uncertain whether he should inform his customer about management's intentions and, thus, risk losing the sale and attendant commission or defer to management's judgment and, thus, possibly salvage the installation.

Scenario 2. A health and beauty aids sales representative confronted the following dilemma. On the last day of the fiscal year, the salesperson was below quota. When calling on a particular customer, this salesperson had an important decision to make. She could oversell the customer and achieve quota; such action, however, could lead to long-run customer dissatisfaction if the customer were unable to move the overstocked merchandise. Alternately, the salesperson could sell the customer only the quantity that was needed; this action would result in the salesperson's failing to obtain quota but maintaining customer satisfaction.

Scenario 3. A real estate agent also faced a potential conflict. He was trying to sell a particular house to one of his clients, who had at last decided to make an offer on the house. The offer was well below the list price of the house, however, and the agent felt confident that the current owner of the home would decline the offer. In hopes of getting his client to make a more acceptable offer, the agent was thinking about telling his client that the seller was presently considering an offer from another potential buyer. In reality, though, no such offer existed.

These vignettes are very realistic for many salespeople. As key links between their organizations and the customer, salespeople encounter situations that may lead to ethical conflict. In fact, previous research has found that salespeople do indeed experience ethical conflict, particularly when the situation is subjective (Dubinsky, Berkowitz, and Rudelius 1980).

Sales management writers (for example, Dalrymple 1982; Futrell 1981a; Russell, Beach, and Buskirk 1978; Stanton and Buskirk 1978) have noted that ethical issues confronting sales personnel can be categorized into two groups: (1) ethics in dealing with customers and (2) ethics in dealing with employers. Customer-related concerns include bribes, gifts, entertainment, reciprocity, and conflicts of interest. Employer-related concerns include moonlighting, relationships with fellow salespeople, use of company assets, expense accounts, and sales contests.

Importance of Resolving Ethical Conflict

Given that salespeople are likely to experience ethical conflict in their jobs, it is incumbent on sales managers to design work environments that mitigate ethical conflict. A failure to assist sales personnel to address ethical dilemmas may leave salespeople bereft of the ability and knowledge necessary to deal effectively with ethical problems. If salespeople do not act in an ethical manner or are unable to resolve ethical dilemmas, the costs to a firm could be significant. For example, being ethically troubled could result in salespeople's experiencing increased levels of job-related tension, frustration, and anxiety; these dysfunctional consequences could further lead to lower job performance and increased turnover (Walker, Churchill, and Ford 1977). Being unable to resolve ethical problems could engender conflict between salespeople and their managers; this result could reduce salespeople's job satisfaction (Walker, Churchill, and Ford 1979). Also, performing the sales job in an unethical or inappropriate fashion may lead to customer dissatisfaction, unfavorable word-of-mouth promotion, as well as reduced sales and profits for the firm. Furthermore, salespeople's acting unethically is a short-run, expedient perspective devoid of any sense of social responsibility (Dodge 1973).

Objectives of Studying Sales Ethics

The preceding discussion suggests that selling ethics is a topic worthy of study by sales practitioners and academics. Research interest in marketing ethics has increased markedly since 1970. (For a critical review of marketing ethics literature, see Murphy and Laczniak, 1981.) Within the sales field, however, only scant research attention has been given to selling ethics. Issues explored include potentially ethically troublesome situations faced by field sales personnel (Dubinsky, Berkowitz, and Rudelius 1980) and retail salespeople (Dubinsky and Levy, in press; Levy and Dubinsky 1983), as well as perceptual differences between industrial sales and purchasing personnel's ethical beliefs (Dubinsky and Gwin 1981).

Currently there is a dearth of literature dealing with a method for examining the ethical problems of field sales personnel. Given the importance of selling ethics, such a method would be useful in assisting sales managers to identify situations that pose ethical problems for their salespeople and to formulate (or revise) policies that address ethical issues confronting their salespeople. This chapter presents a method that sales practitioners can use to explore ethical issues confronting their sales personnel and to design meaningful company policies for dealing with these issues.

Method for Addressing Salespeople's Ethical Problems

Several writers have suggested that companies should develop policies that address employees' ethical problems (Berkman 1977; Boling 1978; Kramer 1977; Rudelius and Bucholz 1979). In fact, Brenner and Molander (1977) found that business people believed that ethics policies or codes may "(a) raise the ethical level of their industry; (b) define the limits of acceptable conduct; and (c) reduce unethical requests" (p. 66). Moreover, Dubinsky, Berkowitz, and Rudelius (1980) determined that field sales personnel appeared to want more guidelines to help them resolve potentially ethically troublesome situations. Thus, the need to develop ethics policies is well founded. The objective of the following method is to identify potentially ethically troublesome situations facing a firm's sales personnel so that operationally useful policies can be established to assist them in resolving their dilemmas. The method for assisting sales practitioners to develop useful ethics guidelines is outlined in the following list and discussed in the following sections.

Step 1: Generate a list of ethical problems.
Step 2: Present items to intra- and extraorganizational members.
Step 3: Create an initial draft of the questionnaire.
Step 4: Conduct a questionnaire pretest.
Step 5: Prepare a final draft of the questionnaire.
Step 6: Administer the questionnaire.
Step 7: Analyze the data.
Step 8: Utilize ethics survey results.
Step 9: Evaluate and communicate policies.

Step 1: Generate a List of Ethical Problems

Sources of Input. The first step in the field sales ethics methodology involves identifying potentially ethically troublesome situations confronting the firm's sales personnel. Identification of these problems is difficult because what may be ethically nettlesome to one individual may be innocuous to another. As Rountree noted:

Each executive has his own individual standards of conduct which he believes to be ethical and these standards are followed. However, ethical standards are set by society and not by individuals. Thus, society evaluates an individual's behavior as ethical or unethical. The problem is that society lacks commonly accepted standards of behavior. Determination of what is right and what is wrong is an extremely difficult task. What is considered ethical conduct varies from country to country, from industry to industry, from situation to situation, and even from person to person. [1976, p. 2]

Because of this problem, input should be obtained from a variety of sources when generating items. By acquiring perceptions from different sources, a panoply of potentially ethically troublesome sales situations can be identified. Intra- and extraorganizational members should be selected to generate items, and these individuals should be in positions that involve interaction with customers and/or sales personnel. At a minimum, salespeople, sales managers, and customers should take part in developing a list of potential ethical dilemmas. These three groups, having different frames of reference, should provide a wealth of information pertaining to ethically troublesome sales situations. Individuals from manufacturing, personnel, credit, purchasing, service, marketing, and other departments involved with sales personnel are additional sources of valuable input in step 1.

Item-Generating Technique. To develop items, an item-generating technique needs to be employed. One mechanism for developing items is the Nominal Group Technique (NGT) (Delbecq, Van De Ven, and Gustafson 1975). Although NGT has been used in only two prior ethics studies (Dubinsky and Levy, in press; Levy and Dubinsky 1983), its use is well documented in the social sciences (Delbecq, Van De Ven, and Gustafson 1975).

NGT would be implemented as follows. First, eight to twelve participants (for example, salespeople, sales managers, and customers) meet with a group moderator to generate, individually and silently, ethical problems salespeople confront on their jobs and to record these problems on paper. Second, the moderator records the participants' situations on a blackboard or flip chart in a round-robin fashion until all situations have been listed. Next, each situation is discussed by group members for purposes of clarification and amplification. Finally, participants vote on the importance of each situation. Those situations receiving a majority of votes constitute the initial set of ethical problems that the company will use in the study.

Group Composition. When using NGT to generate items, the firm must determine the composition of the group. One potential group could consist of a combination of customers, sales managers, and salespeople (or customers, sales managers, salespeople, and individuals from other departments). If this composition is selected, the customer and salesperson participants should not be involved in a business relationship; furthermore, the sales manager participants should not be the supervisors of the salesperson participants. Familiarity between salesperson and customer participants and superior-subordinate relationships between salesperson and sales manager participants could inhibit exchange of ideas during NGT implementation.

An alternative way of implementing NGT would be to use multiple groups of participants; within a given group, participants would be homogeneous (for example, either all customer, all sales manager, or all salesperson participants). Thus, participants in a particular group would have relatively similar frames of references. All groups involved in the NGT process would generate a list of potentially ethically troublesome sales situations. The lists would be merged (and duplicate items deleted) at the conclusion of the NGT process to create the initial set of ethical problems.

Step 2: Present Items to Intra- and Extraorganizational Members

The second step in the field sales methodology entails presenting the initial set of potentially ethically troublesome sales situations generated from NGT to three groups of individuals: customers, sales personnel, and management. Individuals involved in the second step should not have participated in step 1 because these individuals will have been sensitized to the project. The list of items should ideally be presented to participants on a one-on-one basis (as opposed to a group setting) so that the situations can be reviewed with minimum distraction. A relatively small number of customers, salespeople, managers (sales and nonsales) should examine the situations. Management participants should include lower-, middle-, and upper-level sales managers, as well as management personnel from nonsales departments that can markedly impact salespeople's performance (for example, manufacturing, service, credit). The primary purpose of step 2 in this methodology is to supplement and clarify the initial pool of situations generated in step 1. A secondary objective is to help extra- and intraorganizational members acquire an increased awareness of ethical problems confronting company sales personnel.

Step 3: Create an Initial Draft of a Questionnaire

Step 3 of this methodology involves developing an initial draft of a questionnaire that can subsequently be used in surveying company salespeople. The potentially ethically troublesome situations arrived at in the first two steps are included in the questionnaire. The following two questions should be asked for each situation:

1. Do you feel it is a good idea for a firm to have a stated policy that addresses the situation?
2. Does your firm have a stated policy—either written or oral—that addresses the situation?

Responses to question 1 would be recorded on a seven-point scale where 1 = definitely no and 7 = definitely yes. Responses to question 2 would be yes, no, and do not know. These two questions are necessary because responses will assist management to identify the areas in which salespeople want policy help (question 1) and determine whether sales personnel are aware of current company policies (question 2). Situations should be placed on the questionnaire at random to reduce order bias. If management is interested in ascertaining whether salespersons' ethical perceptions differ by type of salesperson, demographic variables such as length of time in present sales position, location of sales territory, kinds of products sold (in multiproduct firms) and salesperson's supervisor would also be included.

Noticeably absent from the questionnaire is a question asking salespeople whether each situation actually presents an ethical question for them. For example, this question could be phrased as follows: Do you believe the situation presents an ethical question for you? That is, do you feel the situation pressures you into taking actions that are inconsistent with what you feel to be right? Although this question would specifically assess whether a given situation is an ethical question for sales personnel, such a question is fraught with problems. Previous research (Levy and Dubinsky 1983) has found that this question leads to respondent misinterpretation; respondents believe that they are being asked whether they would commit the act involved in the situation rather than being asked whether they thought the act was ethically troublesome. Because the issue of question understanding in marketing research is of crucial importance (Peterson, Kerin, and Sabertehrani 1982), a question that directly queries respondents about whether a given situation is ethically troublesome should be excluded from the questionnaire. Question 1 indirectly focuses on this issue by asking respondents whether a company should have a policy that addresses a particular situation. Those situations needing a company policy should presumably be situations that pose ethical problems for salespeople. Conversely, situations not requiring company policy should presumably be situations that do not pose ethical problems for sales personnel. Thus, question 1 should identify selling situations that involve ethical dilemmas for salespeople.

Step 4: Conduct a Questionnaire Pretest

After an initial draft of the questionnaire has been developed, it should be pretested. (For a review of pretesting procedures, see Hunt, Sparkman, and

Wilcox 1982.) The questionnaire should be pretested with a small sample of sales personnel from throughout the sales organization. Although individuals in different positions provided input into identifying potentially ethically troublesome situations facing salespeople, only those individuals on whom the survey is focusing—sales personnel—should be involved in the pretest. Pretest participants should not include salespeople who have been involved in the study up to this point. The major purpose of the pretest is to determine whether salespeople are accurately interpreting items on the questionnaire. Pretest results will then be used in preparing the final draft of the questionnaire.

Step 5: Prepare a Final Draft of the Questionnaire

Based on pretest results, a final draft of the questionnaire is prepared in step 5. In particular, any questions that are ambiguous will be rewritten (and thus clarified) or deleted. Questions that are similar in interpretation will be combined to eliminate redundancy. Items that pretest participants noted are absent from the questionnaire may be added. If major revisions of the questionnaire are made because of pretest results, another pretest should be conducted (Boyd, Westfall, and Stasch 1977). After all questionnaire revisions (and pretests) are concluded, the questionnaire may be administered.

Step 6: Administer the Questionnaire

Step 6 is questionnaire administration. Either a census or a probability sample of the sales force should be generated, depending on the size of the firm. (For a guide to selecting a probability sample, see Churchill 1977.) Each respondent should receive a cover letter explaining the purpose of the study, a questionnaire, and a return envelope provided for convenience. Because the questionnaire addresses a sensitive issue—ethics in field sales—anonymity should be promised in the cover letter; failure to do so may well result in a low response rate and/or socially acceptable responses. In fact, Futrell (1981b) found that when a survey addresses sensitive issues, absence of anonymity can produce measurement error and response bias. To reduce these adverse effects, he recommended that the cover letter promise anonymity and the questionnaire be administered by someone external to the firm, like a management consultant. The cover letter should also indicate a date by which the questionnaire is to be returned. Providing a date allows sales personnel to allocate time in their work schedules for completion of the questionnaire.

Step 7: Analyze the Data

This step entails analyzing the data contained in the completed questionnaires. (For a discussion about issues to consider when selecting data analysis techniques and about different kinds of data analysis techniques, see Churchill 1977). In this step management should again consider the purpose of the study: to identify where salespeople want policy help. Management should keep this purpose in mind when analyzing the data. The data analysis should employ techniques that will assist management in achieving the objective of the study. Also, if management had established a priori hypotheses prior to questionnaire design and administration, then appropriate data analysis techniques should be used to examine the status of each hypothesis (its acceptance or rejection).

Step 8: Utilize Ethics Survey Results

The eighth step in the field sales ethics methodology is utilizing the results of the study. Management carefully examines the results of the survey. Management notes the situations on which sales personnel tend to want policy help and situations for which they are aware or unaware of current company policy. The results of this analysis suggest what managerial action must be taken to assist salespeople to address ethical problems. More specifically, survey findings indicate where policies must be clarified, added, or even deleted and where current policies must be clearly communicated to sales personnel.

For example, survey results may indicate that salespeople want a policy to address the issue of giving gifts or free entertainment to customers where no policy presently focuses on this issue. Consequently, a policy could be formulated that deals with this problem. Study findings might reveal that a current policy pertaining to back-door selling is too restrictive. Management, therefore, may wish to modify the policy to make it more amenable to salespeople's needs by providing them with opportunity to employ such a selling strategy with appropriate discretion. The data could suggest that a particular policy covering expense account padding is now irrelevant because management currently requires submission of receipts for all business expenditures. Thus, the policy could be deleted. Or results of the survey may show that most salespeople want a policy to address the issue of when (or if) the company car may be driven for personal use, but few salespersons know that a policy currently deals with this problem. As a result, this policy needs to be clearly communicated to sales personnel. Management should be mindful that when making policy changes, the changes should be made in concert with the legal department to ensure that the changes will not pose legal problems.

After management has developed ethical guidelines for the sales force, it should introduce the policies to sales personnel. When implementing its actions, management should not present its ethical policies to the sales force in the form of a company edict; rather, the policies should be integrated into the organization by explaining their importance and rationale to the salespeople. Through this explication and justification, management hopes the salespeople will discover that the policies are designed to assist them in the performance of their job and, thereby, to internalize the policies into their sales positions. Policies could be presented to sales personnel via group meetings with management, one-on-one informal sessions between a salesperson and his or her immediate supervisor, or a special sales training session. This same information must be presented to new salespeople when they assume their positions.

Step 9: Evaluate and Communicate Policies

The last step in the field sales ethics methodology is to assess periodically the impact of the firm's ethics policies and to articulate the policies to concerned parties. In particular, management must track the success of written policies in helping sales personnel solve ethical questions. When new problems arise, they should trigger the development of written policies. When existing guidelines become inappropriate or too cumbersome, they should be modified or dropped.

Also, policies must be communicated periodically to all those affected inside and outside the firm—namely, to both sales personnel and customers. Communicating the policies to salespeople is critical to remind them of what company guidelines are. Research (Dubinsky, Berkowitz, and Rudelius 1980) has highlighted the necessity of such communication by noting that sales personnel from within the same firm may be unsure whether their company has a policy addressing a particular ethically troublesome situation. Thus, review sessions that articulate company policies to all salespeople should be conducted periodically. Informing customers of the policies should also serve to reduce the chances of ethical conflict between the firm's customers and salespeople.

Managerial Guidelines

Possible ethical situations confronted by salespeople that could be studied using this methodology are shown in table 4–1. According to research conducted by this writer and a colleague (Levy and Dubinsky 1983), the thirty-one situations have been classified using the procedure outlined here. Although these situations relate to department store and specialty store retail salespeople, many of them are experienced by manufacturers' representatives and industrial salespersons.

The data in table 4–1 can be explained more fully:

Specifically, the first eighteen situations represent customer-related situations; the next eight [are] work-related situations; the last five [are] peer-related situations. In addition, the situations within each of the three categories are arranged in descending order based upon department store salespeople's mean

Table 4–1
Perceptions of Whether Situation Should Be Addressed by Company Policy[a]

Situation	Department Store Salespeople		Specialty Store Salespeople	
	Mean[b]	S.D.	Mean[b]	S.D.
Customer-related situations				
1. Pressure customers into making a purchase.	6.7	(1.11)	6.5	(1.21)
2. Customer damages product in the store and wants a markdown.	6.7	(1.01)	6.2[c]	(1.56)
3. Give incorrect change to customers on purpose.	6.7	(1.32)	6.1[c]	(1.86)
4. Charge full price for a sale item without the customer's knowledge.	6.5	(1.41)	5.8[c]	(1.94)
5. Charge markdown price to customers for similar full-price merchandise.	6.4	(1.39)	5.9	(1.72)
6. Take return from customer when you think the item should not be accepted.	6.4	(1.50)	6.3	(1.37)
7. Refuse return by customer when you think the item should be accepted.	6.3	(1.58)	6.2	(1.60)
8. Make a promise that you cannot keep regarding the time when something will be ready.	6.1	(1.62)	6.0	(1.93)
9. Hoard free samples that are meant for customers.	5.9	(1.74)	5.6	(1.96)
10. Make excuses when merchandise is not ready for customer to pick up.	5.6	(1.70)	5.1	(2.01)
11. Ignore a prospective customer for one you believe will be better one.	5.6	(1.88)	5.4	(2.05)
12. Don't offer information about an upcoming sale that will include merchandise the customer is planning to buy.	5.5	(1.98)	5.1	(2.02)
13. Don't tell the complete truth to a customer about the characteristics of a product.	5.5	(1.94)	5.8	(1.76)
14. Don't assist customers you believe are less likely to buy.	5.5	(2.04)	5.6	(2.06)
15. Make excuses to customers about unavailable merchandise that is not yet in stock or is sold out.	5.4	(1.92)	5.1	(2.03)
16. Buy merchandise before it is available to the customer.	4.9	(2.35)	4.2	(2.35)
17. Give preferential treatment to certain customers.	4.7	(2.27)	4.4	(2.28)
18. Sell a more expensive product when a less expensive one would be better for the customer.	4.7	(2.38)	4.2	(2.20)
Work-related situations				
19. Sign time sheet incorrectly for time worked.	6.7	(1.03)	6.4	(1.48)
20. Don't get a check authorization when required.	6.5	(1.36)	6.6	(1.26)
21. Have to sell nonsale items at full price when the items were accidently placed with sale merchandise.	6.3	(1.33)	5.6[c]	(1.98)

Table 4–1 continued

Situation	Department Store Salespeople		Specialty Store Salespeople	
	Mean[b]	S.D.	Mean[b]	S.D.
22. Perform your job with inadequate job information or training.	6.3	(1.45)	6.1	(1.66)
23. Hide merchanise that you want and are waiting for the store to mark down.	6.1	(1.76)	6.0	(1.75)
24. Sell the product as an exclusive, when in fact it is available in other stores.	5.0	(2.04)	5.0	(2.11)
25. Don't sell the last unit because you want to purchase it yourself.	5.0	(2.28)	5.1	(2.18)
26. Use of a sales contest for sales associates in order to generate sales to customers.	4.8	(2.17)	5.4	(2.03)
Peer-related situations				
27. Pressure from a friend or family member not entitled to a discount to give him or her your employee discount.	6.8	(0.88)	6.3[c]	(1.42)
28. Offer to give a friend (or family member) not entitled to a discount your employee discount.	6.6	(1.15)	6.1	(1.54)
29. Take sales away from sales associate.	6.0	(1.89)	6.2	(1.76)
30. Pressure from fellow sales associates not to report theft.	4.8	(2.24)	4.3	(2.30)
31. Peer pressure not to say anything to management about other sales associates' personal problems.	4.3	(2.07)	3.5	(2.18)

Source: Levy, M. and Dubinsky, A.J., "Identifying and Addressing Retail Salespeople's Ethical Problems: A Method and Application," *Journal of Retailing* Vol. 59 (Spring 1983), pp. 57–58. Reprinted with permission.

[a]Salespeople's perceptions are based on the question, Do you feel it is a good idea for a firm to have a stated policy that addresses the situation?

[b]Mean scores are based on a 7-point scale where 1 means "Definitely no" and 7 means "Definitely yes."

[c]$p \leq .05$.

scores. The higher the ranking of a situation, the more strongly department store salespeople feel that the situation should be addressed by policy.

Of the thirty-one situations, five exhibit significant differences between the perceptions of the two retail sales groups. In all five situations, department store sales personnel believe more strongly than do specialty store personnel that the situation should be addressed by policy. Three of the five situations are customer-related. They are: being asked to give a markdown on a product the customer has damaged (situation 2); giving incorrect change to a customer (situation 3); and charging full price for a sale item (situation 4). One of the situations exhibiting a significant difference is work-related: selling a nonsale item that was placed with sale items at full price (situation 21). And one of the five situations is peer-related: feeling pressure to give an employee discount (situation 27). A potential reason for the divergent perceptions of the two sales groups may be the substantially different work situation in which the two groups operate (for example, types of products sold, types of customers reached, extant span of control). [Levy and Dubinsky 1983, pp. 56 and 59]

Conclusion

The proposed methodology for studying field salespeople's ethical problems can provide a wealth of information to managers interested in designing useful company guidelines. The methodology should indicate for management where sales personnel want policy help, how well management is communicating current company policies, and what policies need modification. From this kind of analysis, sales managers should be able to develop policies that assist salespeople in addressing effectively the ethical problems they confront in their jobs. The end result should be an improved work environment in which sales personnel operate.

References

Berkman, H.W. 1977. "Corporate Ethics: Who Cares?" *Journal of the Academy of Marketing Science* 5 (Summer), pp. 154–167.

Boling, T.E. 1978. "The Management Ethics 'Crisis': An Organizational Perspective." *Academy of Management Review* 3 (April), pp. 360–365.

Boyd, H.W., R. Westfall, and S.F. Stasch. 1977. *Marketing Research: Text and Cases*. Homewood, Ill.: Richard D. Irwin, Inc.

Brenner, S.N., and E.A. Molander. 1977. "Is the Ethics of Business Changing?" *Harvard Business Review* 55 (January-February), pp. 57–71.

Churchill, G.A. 1976. *Marketing Research: Methodological Foundations*. Hinsdale, Ill.: Dryden Press.

Dalrymple, D.J. 1982. *Sales Management: Concepts and Cases*. New York: John Wiley & Sons.

Delbecq, A.L., A.H. Van De Ven, and D.H. Gustafson. 1975. *Group Techniques for Program Planning: A Guide to Nominal Group and Delphi Processes*. Glenview, Ill.: Scott Foresman and Company.

Dodge, H.R. 1973. *Field Sales Management: Text and Cases*. Dallas: Business Publications, Inc.

Dubinsky, A.J., E.N. Berkowitz, and W. Rudelius. 1980. "Ethical Problems of Field Sales Personnel." *MSU Business Topics* 28 (Summer), pp. 11–16.

Dubinsky, A.J., and J.M. Gwin. 1981. "Business Ethics: Buyers and Sellers." *Journal of Purchasing and Materials Management* 17 (Winter), pp. 9–16.

Dubinsky, A.J., and M. Levy. Forthcoming. "Ethics in Retailing: Perceptions of Retail Salespeople." *Journal of the Academy of Marketing Science*.

Futrell, C. 1981a. *Sales Management: Behavior, Practice and Cases*. Hinsdale, Ill.: Dryden Press.

———. 1981b. "Effects of Signed versus Unsigned Attitudes Questionnaires." *Journal of the Academy of Marketing Science* 9 (Winter/Spring), pp. 93–102.

Hunt, S.D., R.D. Sparkman, Jr., and J.B. Wilcox. 1982. "The Pretest in Survey Research: Issues and Preliminary Findings." *Journal of Marketing Research* 19 (May), pp. 269–273.

Kramer, O.P. 1977. "Ethics Programs Can Help Companies Set Standards of Content." *Administrative Management* 38 (January), pp. 46–49.

Levy, M., and A.J. Dubinsky. 1983. "Identifying and Addressing Retail Salespeople's Ethical Problems: A Method and Application." *Journal of Retailing* 59 (Spring), pp. 46–66.

Murphy, P.E., and G.R. Laczniak. 1981. "Marketing Ethics: A Review with Implications for Managers, Educators, and Researchers." In *Review of Marketing 1981*, B.M. Enis and K.J. Roering, eds. Chicago: American Marketing Association.

Peterson, R.A., R.S. Kerin, and M. Sabertehrani. 1982. "Question Understanding in Self-Report Data." In *AMA Educators' Conference Proceedings*, B.J. Walker et al., eds. Chicago: American Marketing Association.

Rountree, W.D. 1976. *Ethical Aspects of Personal Selling*. Boone, N.C.: Appalachian State University, College of Business.

Rudelius, W., and R.A. Bucholz. 1979. "Ethical Problems of Purchasing Managers." *Harvard Business Review* 57 (March-April), pp. 8–17.

Russell, F.A., F.H. Beach, and R.H. Buskirk. 1978. *Textbook of Salesmanship*. New York: McGraw-Hill Book Company.

Stanton, W.J., and R.H. Buskirk. 1978. *Management of the Sales Force*. Homewood, Ill.: Richard D. Irwin, Inc.

Walker, O.C., G.A. Churchill, and N.M. Ford. 1977. "Motivation and Performance in Industrial Selling: Present Knowledge and Needed Research." *Journal of Marketing Research* 14 (May), pp. 156–168.

———. 1979. "Where Do We Go from Here? Selected Conceptual and Empirical Issues Concerning the Motivation and Performance of the Industrial Salesforce." In *Critical Issues in Sales Management: State-of-the-Art and Future Research Needs*, G. Albaum and G.A. Churchill, eds. Eugene: College of Business Administration, University of Oregon.

5
Ethical Issues in Marketing Research

Donald S. Tull
Del I. Hawkins

I s it ethical to secure information from individuals that they are unwilling to provide? Should opinions be elicited that the respondent does not want to give? Questions like these—ethical questions—are often ignored in marketing research (Murphy and Laczniak 1981). However, many ethical questions are involved in the marketing research process. Figure 5–1 presents several specific research practices that some individuals might view as being less than completely ethical.

It is essential that marketing research students, practitioners, and professors develop an awareness of and concern for the ethical issues of the profession. The process of studying and practicing a profession can apparently alter an individual's perceptions of the rights and prerogatives of that profession. For example, evidence suggests that the pursuit of a business education leads to more tolerant attitudes toward questionable business practices than those held by students with other majors (Hawkins and Cocanougher 1972; Gelb and Brien 1971; Shuptrine 1979). Likewise, salespeople have shown more tolerance for such activities than students (Dubinsky and Rudelius 1980).

If these findings are correct, the person engaging in marketing research may unknowingly use techniques and practices that the general public considers unethical. Therefore, we should examine this field for activities that may be questionable in the view of the general public. Such an examination should lead to research practices in line with the general ethical expectations of society. This approach is not only good in some absolute sense but also self-serving. Most of us would prefer to maintain high standards of conduct voluntarily rather than have standards set and enforced by governmental action. For example, the Privacy Act of 1974 requires that each respondent in a federal government survey be explicitly informed, both verbally and in writing, of (1) whether the survey is voluntary or mandatory, (2) the purpose of the survey, (3) how the information is to be used, and (4) the conse-

Figure 5–1. Specific Research Practices with Ethical Implications

1. Research has consistently found that including a small amount of money in a mail survey will greatly increase the response rate. Promises of money for returning the questionnaire are much less effective. One explanation is that respondents experience guilt if they do not complete a questionnaire for which they have already been "paid," but find it not worth their while to complete a questionnaire for the amount of money usually promised. Based on this, a research firm puts 25¢ in all its mail surveys.

2. A research firm specializes in telephone surveys. It recently began using voice pitch analysis in an attempt to determine if respondents were distorting their answers to sensitive questions.

3. A mall intercept facility recently installed hidden eye-tracking equipment. Now, when respondents are asked to view advertisements or packages, they are not told that their eye movements are being recorded.

4. The research director of a large corporation is convinced that using the company's name in surveys with consumers produces (1) lowered response rates and (2) distorted answers. Therefore, the firm routinely conducts surveys using the title, Public Opinion Institute.

5. A company dramatically cuts the price of its products in a city where a competitor is test marketing a new product.

6. An insurance company uses a variety of projective techniques to assist in preparing advertisements for life insurance. Potential respondents are told that the purpose of the tests is to isolate factors that influence creativity.

7. A survey finds that 80 percent of the doctors responding do not recommend any particular brand of margarine to their patients who are concerned about cholesterol. Five per cent recommend Brand A, four per cent recommend Brand B, and no other brand is recommended by over 2 per cent of the doctors. The company runs an advertisement that states: "More doctors recommend Brand A margarine for cholesterol control than any other brand."

---

quences to the individual of not participating in the survey. Few commercial researchers would welcome this level of control.

A final benefit from a highly ethical approach to the marketing research process is improved public acceptance. The essential nature of public acceptance is clear:

> Let's face it, we are able to collect our research data only because the general public continues to be willing to submit to our interviews. This acceptance of us by the public is the basic natural resource on which our industry is built. Without it, we would be out of business tomorrow. [Carlson 1967, p. 5]

Unfortunately, we do not have a list of ethical and unethical marketing practices that covers all the situations the marketing researcher may face. Several issues are controversial within the profession (Crawford 1970; Smith 1979; Tybout and Zaltman 1974, 1975; Day 1975). Some widely accepted social values like the individual's right to privacy support one position, whereas equally accepted values like the individual's right to seek knowledge may support an opposing position.

This chapter examines the nature of ethics in marketing research and discusses specific ethical issues. A brief treatment of corporate espionage is also provided.

The Nature of Ethical Issues in Marketing Research

Models for ethics in the general field of marketing have been proposed by a number of authors (McMahon 1968; Hollander 1974; Frey and Kinnear 1979). Each of these models provides useful insights and a general guide for action. However, none of the models is specific enough to provide an unambiguous guide to behavior in specific marketing research situations.

The AMA provides a Marketing Research Code of Ethics, which is reproduced in figure 5–2. This code is an excellent starting point, but it leaves some of the crucial issues untouched.

Four distinct groups are affected by the research process: (1) the general public, (2) the respondents in the specific study, (3) the client, and (4) the researcher. Specific ethical issues relating to each of these groups are presented.

Protection of the Public

A true professional focuses first on the needs of the public or innocent third parties. A falsified research report used to justify funding for the client by a bank would be unethical (and illegal), despite the fact that it might be economically advantageous to both the researcher and the client. Three major areas of concern arise in this context (each of the three can also influence the client-researcher relationship): incomplete reporting, misleading reporting, and nonobjective research. These areas are closely interrelated in their effects.

Incomplete Reporting. A client requesting that information that could be harmful to the sale of a product not be included in a research report to be released to the public is analogous to a seller of a product not disclosing potentially damaging information about a product in a sales presentation to the buyer. Both are attempts to mislead potential buyers by leaving them uninformed about undesirable features or characteristics of the product.

There are no legal requirements about failure to disclose negative information in research reports to be released to the public. There are clear ethical requirements to do so, however, and the reputable researcher will ensure that such information is included.

Misleading Reporting. Closely related to incomplete reporting is misleading reporting. Misleading reporting involves presenting the research results in such

Figure 5-2. Marketing Research Code of Ethics

The American Marketing Association, in furtherance of its central objective of the advancement of science in marketing and in recognition of its obligation to the public, has established these principles of ethical practice of marketing research for the guidance of its members. In an increasingly complex society, marketing management is more and more dependent upon marketing information intelligently and systematically obtained. The consumer is the source of much of this information. Seeking the cooperation of the consumer in the development of information, marketing management must acknowledge its obligation to protect the public from misrepresentation and exploitation under the guise of research.

Similarly, the research practitioner has an obligation to the discipline and to those who provide support for it—an obligation to adhere to basic and commonly accepted standards of scientific investigation as they apply to the domain of marketing research.

It is the intent of this code to define ethical standards required of marketing research in satisfying these obligations.

Adherence to this code will assure the users of marketing research that the research was done in accordance with acceptable ethical practices. Those engaged in research will find in this code an affirmation of sound and honest basic principles which have developed over the years as the profession has grown. The field interviewers who are the point of contact between the profession and the consumer will also find guidance in fulfilling their vitally important role.

For Research Users, Practitioners, and Interviewers

1. No individual or organization will undertake any activity which is directly or indirectly represented to be marketing research, but which has as its real purpose the attempted sale of merchandise or services to some or all of the respondents interviewed in the course of the research.

2. If respondents have been led to believe, directly or indirectly, that they are participating in a marketing research survey and that their anonymity will be protected, their names shall not be made known to anyone outside the research organization or research department, or used for other than research purposes.

For Research Practitioners

1. There will be no intentional or deliberate misrepresentation of research methods or results. An adequate description of methods employed will be made available upon request to the sponsor of the research. Evidence that fieldwork has been completed according to specifications will, upon request, be made available to buyers of research.

2. The identity of the survey sponsor and/or the ultimate client for whom a survey is being done will be held in confidence at all times, unless this identity is to be revealed as part of the research design. Research information shall be held in confidence by the research organization or department and not used for personal gain or made available to any outside party unless the client specifically authorizes such release.

Figure 5–2 continued

---

3. A research organization shall not undertake marketing studies for competitive clients when such studies would jeopardize the confidential nature of client-agency relationships.

For Users of Marketing Research

1. A user of research shall not knowingly disseminate conclusions from a given research project or service that are inconsistent with or not warranted by the data.

2. To the extent that there is involved in a research project a unique design involving techniques, approaches, or concepts not commonly available to research practitioners, the prospective user of research shall not solicit such a design from one practitioner and deliver it to another for execution without the approval of the design originator.

For Field Interviewers

1. Research assignments and materials received, as well as information obtained from respondents, shall be held in confidence by the interviewer and revealed to no one except the research organization conducting the marketing study.

2. No information gained through a marketing research activity shall be used, directly or indirectly, for the personal gain or advantage of the interviewer.

3. Interviews shall be conducted in strict accordance with specifications and instructions received.

4. An interviewer shall not carry out two or more interviewing assignments simultaneously, unless authorized by all contractors or employers concerned.

Members of the American Marketing Association will be expected to conduct themselves in accordance with the provisions of this code in all of their marketing research activities.

Reprinted with permission from the American Marketing Association. Minor editorial changes have been made that do not affect the meaning.

a manner that the intended audience will draw a conclusion that is not justified by the results. This sometimes occurs when research results are used in advertising campaigns.

For example, a recent ad claimed that following comparison tests, "an amazing 60 percent" of a sample of consumers said that Triumph cigarettes tasted as good or better than Merit. This was indeed indicated by the results. However, since many respondents said the brands tasted the same (as good as), the results also indicated that 64 percent said that Merit tasted as good or better than Triumph (Diamond 1982). The public presentation of these results would most likely mislead a substantial portion of the general public. Figure 5–3 provides a more detailed example of misleading reporting of research results.

Figure 5–3. Misleading Presentation of Marketing Research in in Advertising Copy

The prototype commercial featured a well-known high fashion model saying: "In shampoo tests with over 900 women like me, *Body on Tap* got higher ratings than *Prell* for body. Higher than *Flex* for conditioning. Higher than *Sassoon* for strong, healthy-looking hair."

The evidence showed that several groups of approximately 200 women each tested just one shampoo. They rated it on a six-step scale, from "outstanding" to "poor," for 27 separate attributes, such as body and conditioning. Nine hundred women did not, after trying both shampoos, make product-to-product comparisons between *Body on Tap* and *Sassoon* or between *Body on Tap* and any of the other brands mentioned. In fact, no woman in the tests tried more than one shampoo.

The basis for the claim that the women preferred *Body on Tap* to *Sassoon* for "strong, healthy looking hair" was to combine the data for the "outstanding" and "excellent" ratings and discard the lower four ratings on the scale. The figures then were 36 per cent for *Body on Tap* and 24 per cent (of a separate group of women) for *Sassoon*. When the "very good" and "good" ratings were combined with the "outstanding" and "excellent" ratings, however, there was only an insignificant difference of 1 per cent between the two products in the category of "strong, healthy looking hair."

The research was conducted for Bristol-Myers by Marketing Information Systems, Inc. (MISI), using a technique known as blind monadic testing. The president of MISI testified that this method typically is employed when what is wanted is an absolute response to a product "without reference to another specific product." Although he testified that blind monadic testing was used in connection with comparative advertising, that was not the purpose for which Bristol-Myers retained MISI. Rather, they wished to determine consumer reaction to the introduction of *Body on Tap*.

Sassoon also found some other things wrong with the tests and the way they were represented to the Bristol-Myers advertisements. The fashion model said 900 women "like me" tried the shampoos. Actually, one-third of the women were aged 13 to 18. This was significant because *Body on Tap* appealed disproportionately to teenagers, and the advertising executive who created the campaign for Bristol-Myers testified that its purpose was to attract a large portion of the *adult* women's shampoo market.

Sassoon commissioned its own research to support its legal position. ASI Market Research, Inc. screened the *Body on Tap* commercial, along with other material, for a group of 635 women and then asked them several questions individually.

Some 95 per cent of those who responded said each of the 900 women referred to in the commercial had tried two or more brands. And 62 per cent said that the tests showed [that] *Body on Tap* was competitively superior.

Source: S.A. Diamond, "Market Research Latest Target in Ad Claims," *Advertising Age*, January 25, 1982, p. 52. Used with permission.

Nonobjective Research. The researcher, the client, or both would often benefit if certain research findings were obtained. There is no doubt that the "intention or deliberate misrepresentation of research methods or results," specified in the AMA code, is unethical. However, research techniques can be selected to maximize the likelihood of obtaining a given finding.

The ease of using relatively standard techniques in a nonobjective way can be seen in the following example. A small community wishes to attract retail outlets from several chain stores. A researcher is hired to develop a presentation to the managements of the chains. The researcher realizes that the chain stores weigh per capita income very heavily in their location decisions. However, the community concerned is quite poor, except for a very few people who are quite wealthy. The researcher therefore takes a census of the population and computes an average income figure. This is not incorrect from a technical point of view. However, a median rather than an average income figure would give a more realistic picture of the community's income as it relates to the decision at hand.

Protection of Respondents

Two ethical issues confront researchers in their relationship with respondents—namely, the use of the guise of conducting a survey to sell products and the invasion of the privacy of the respondent.

Use of Marketing Research Guise to Sell Products. The use of the statement, "I am conducting a survey," as a guise for sales presentations or to obtain information for sales leads is a major concern of legitimate researchers. Both telephone and personal interviews have been used for sales solicitation. Some mail surveys may have served to generate sales leads or mailing lists. Although the public still appears to support legitimate surveys, the widespread incidence of phony interviews could change this essential acceptance. Fortunately, this practice is illegal as well as unethical (Frey and Kinnear 1980, pp. 296–298).

Invasion of Privacy of Respondents. The right to privacy refers to the public's general feeling or perception of its ability to restrict the amount of personal data it will make available to outsiders. The three important elements involved in this right are the concept of privacy, the concept of informed consent by which an individual can waive the right to privacy, and the concept that anonymity and confidentiality can help protect those whose privacy has, to some extent, been invaded (U.S. Executive Office of the President 1967).

The right to privacy. This is the right of individuals to decide for themselves how much of their thoughts, feelings, and the facts of their personal lives they will share with others. It is the right to live one's life in one's own way, to formulate and hold one's own beliefs, and to express thoughts and share feelings without fear of observation or publicity beyond that which one seeks or in which one acquiesces.

What is private varies between individuals and within individuals from day to day and setting to setting. The essence of the concept is the right of each individual to decide in each particular setting or compartment of his or her life how much to reveal. It appears that the general public is becoming more concerned with the right to privacy (Goldfield 1977). This may reflect a concern about having personal data placed in a computer data bank as well as a decrease in trust in both business and government.

Because the essence of the right of privacy is the individual's ability to choose what will be revealed, the marketing researcher must not abrogate the respondent's ability to choose. This requires the researcher to obtain the free and informed consent of the potential respondents. Free consent implies that the potential respondent is not encumbered by any real or imagined pressure to participate in the study other than a desire to cooperate or contribute.

In practice, informed means providing potential respondents with sufficient information for them to determine whether participation is worthwhile and desirable, from their point of view. This would, in general, involve a description of the types of questions to be asked or the task required, the subject areas covered, the time and physical effort involved, and the ultimate use to which the resultant data will be put.

Few requests for cooperation for marketing research studies convey all this information. However, several studies on the effect of providing full information, including statements stressing the respondent's right not to participate, have found these procedures to have no or minimal effects on the overall response rate, item response rate, or the nature of the obtained responses (Singer 1978a; Hawkins 1979). In addition, these procedures do not appear to affect the respondents' evaluation of the interview (Singer 1978b).

Some marketing studies and techniques may be less able to withstand full disclosure. Disguised techniques are based on the premise that more accurate or meaningful answers can be obtained if the respondent is not aware of the purpose of the questions. As Bogart stated, "Must we really explain, when we ask the respondent to agree or disagree with the statement, 'Prison is too good for sex criminals; they should be publicly whipped or worse,' that it is really the authoritarianism of his personality we are investigating and not public opinion on crime and punishment" (1962, p. 9)?

Informed consent does not seem to require the level of detail suggested in this quote. However, it does require that the respondent be told that some of the questions during the interview will be used to measure certain aspects of personality. Similarly, when projective techniques are being used, the respondent can be told that some responses will be analyzed to reveal underlying attitudes on certain topics. Such information seems sufficient to allow the respondents to decide if they wish to participate.

To the extent that fully informed consent cannot be obtained, anonymity and confidentiality are important. Anonymity means that the identity of the subject is never known to anyone. Confidentiality means that the respondent's identity is known at one point in time to only a limited number of investigators but is otherwise protected from dissemination.

The right to seek knowledge. In the preceding paragraphs, emphasis was given to the right of privacy of the respondent. However, the right to learn or to seek knowledge is also valued highly in our society. The right of the researcher to learn about human behavior and its causes is definitely restricted by the preceding view of the right of privacy. An alternative view, which focuses more on the rights of the researcher, can be labeled the *no harm, no foul* approach. The view of privacy that has been presented is based on the proposition that the researcher must refrain from engaging in any activity to which the respondents might object if they knew its exact nature, even though they do not object to it with current knowledge.

A competing view is that the researcher should feel free to conduct any study that does not harm the respondents physically or psychologically. Thus, the fact that a respondent would object to revealing the real reasons for purchasing a certain product should not deter the researcher from using projective techniques to uncover these reasons. The respondents react to a series of vague stimuli and leave feeling that they have helped in a research project and perhaps feeling that researchers are a little weird for showing such strange pictures. The researcher has data that allow an understanding of subconscious purchase motives. If the research is competently done, the final result is a better product, more meaningful advertising, more efficient distribution, or a more appropriate price.

This approach requires strict attention to anonymity and confidentiality but does not require informed consent. It does not suggest that respondents be abused, deceived unnecessarily, or pressured into cooperating. It does maintain the position that no physical or psychological harm occur to the respondent. Essentially this position is that one's privacy cannot be invaded if one is unaware of the invasion and the invasion causes no harm.

Protection of the Client

Every professional has the obligation to protect the client in matters relating to their professional relationship. The marketing researcher is no exception. The issues concerning matters in which the client may expect protection when authorizing a marketing research project include protection against

(1) abuse of position arising from specialized knowledge, (2) unnecessary research, (3) an unqualified researcher, (4) disclosure of identity, (5) treating data as nonconfidential and/or nonproprietary, and (6) misleading presentation of data.

Abuse of Position. The marketing manager is usually at a substantial disadvantage in discussing a research project. Most researchers have specialized knowledge and experience that the marketing manager cannot match. Therefore, the manager is frequently forced to accept the researcher's suggestions at face value, just as we often accept the advice of medical doctors or lawyers. Like other professionals, the marketing researcher often has the opportunity to take advantage of specialized knowledge to the detriment of the client.

Of particular concern in this area is the opportunity, and the temptation, to use faulty research designs and/or methodological shortcuts to meet time or cost constraints. The concern in this area is with practices such as applying pressure, financial or otherwise, on the interviewers to obtain a high response rate in short time periods and then not using a verification procedure to ensure that the interviews were actually done. Another example is using a new questionnaire without adequate pretesting.

Unnecessary Research. Researchers are frequently requested to engage in a specific research project that is unrelated to the underlying problem, has been done before, or is economically unjustified. The researcher can often benefit from such an activity. This gain frequently exceeds whatever goodwill might be generated by refusing to conduct unwarranted research. Should the researcher accept such assignments?

A sales representative may not feel obligated to be certain that the customer really needs the product (although a careful application of the marketing concept requires it). But a doctor or lawyer is ethically prohibited from prescribing unwarranted medicine or legal action. This issue is not addressed in the AMA code of ethics. However, it seems to these writers that the researcher has a professional obligation to indicate to the client that, in his or her judgment, the research expenditure is not warranted. If, after this judgment has been clearly stated, the client still desires the research, the researcher can never know for certain the risk preferences and strategies that are guiding the client's behavior.

Unqualified Researchers. Another area of concern involves the request for research that is beyond the capabilities or technical expertise of the individual researcher or research organization. The cost, both psychological and economic, of saying "I cannot do this as well as some other individual" can be quite high. However, accepting a project beyond the researcher's capacities typically results in time delays, higher costs, and decreased accuracy.

Again, professional ethics should compel the researcher to indicate to the potential client the fact that the research requires the application of techniques that are outside his or her area of expertise. If the researcher feels capable of completing this project, there is every right to attempt to convince the client of this. However, if the task is not one that the researcher can reasonably expect to perform well, a more suitable researcher should be suggested.

Anonymity of Client. The client will have authorized a marketing research project either to help identify or solve marketing problems. In either case, it may well be to the advantage of competitors to know that the study is being done. The researcher is therefore obligated ethically to preserve the anonymity of the client. The fact that a particular firm is sponsoring a study should not be revealed to any outside party unless the client so agrees. This includes respondents and other existing and potential clients.

Confidential and Proprietary Information. The data generated for a particular client and the conclusion and interpretations from those data are the exclusive property of the client. It is obvious that a researcher should not turn over a client's study to one of the client's competitors. However, what if the researcher gathers basic demographic material on a geographic area for one client and the same information is required for a study by a noncompeting client? The AMA code is not clear on this point, but it seems to suggest that such data cannot be used twice without the explicit consent of the original client. Reuse of the data, assuming that permission is granted, should result in the two clients' sharing the cost of this aspect of the research rather than the research organization's charging twice. A research agency should not conduct studies for competitive clients if there is a possibility that this would jeopardize the confidential nature of the client-agency relationship.

Misleading Presentations of Data. Reports that are presented orally or are written in such a way as to give deliberately the impression of greater accuracy than the data warrant are obviously not in the best interest of the client. Such an impression can be left by reports by a number of means. These include the use of overly technical jargon, failure to round numbers properly, unnecessary use of the complex analytic procedures, and incomplete reporting.

Overly Technical Jargon. All specialties tend to develop a unique terminology. By and large, this is useful because it allows those familiar with the field to communicate in a more concise and precise way. However, technical jargon and extensive mathematical notation can also convey a false aura of complexity and precision. The research report's primary function is to convey to the client the results of the research. It is not the proper place to demonstrate the complexity of sampling formulas or the range of terms that is unique to the research process.

Failure to Round Numbers Properly. An impression of greater precision than the data warrant can also be created through the failure to round numbers properly. For example, a statement that the average annual expenditure by some group for furniture is $261.17 implies more precision than is normally warranted. If the reseacher believes that the data are accurate to the nearest $10, the average should be rounded to $260. If the data were developed for a sample, the use of a confidence interval might be appropriate as well.

Unnecessary Use of Complex Analytic Procedures. The transformation of the data into logarithms when they could just as well be analyzed in arithmetic form and the normalizing of data when they would be better left in nonnormalized states are examples of needlessly complex analytic procedures. When necessary, the use of such procedures is confusing at best and misleading at worst.

Incomplete Reporting. Incomplete reporting renders an objective appraisal of the research report impossible. It can create false impressions of the accuracy of the research or even of the meaning of the resultant data. Both the initial client and any concerned third party have a right to expect a report that will allow them to make a reasonable assessment of the accuracy of the data.

An example should make this point clear. Assume that a sample is drawn from a population of 10,000 individuals and the final report shows an obtained sample size of 750. On the surface, this may appear to be a very reasonable sample size. However, unless other descriptive data are given, there is no way to estimate the potential impact of nonresponse error. An evaluation of the probable effects of this source of error requires a knowledge of the response rate. The 750 respondents could represent a response rate as low as 10 or 20 percent or as high as 100 percent. One's confidence in the resulting data (depending, of course, on the nature of the data), would vary considerably between these two extremes. One guide to what should be presented in a research report, from an ethical standpoint, is presented in figure 5–4.

Protection of the Research Firm

Several issues can arise in the research firm–client relationship in which the research organization needs protection. These include protection against improper solicitation of proposals, disclosure of proprietary information on techniques, and misrepresentation of findings.

Improper Solicitation of Proposals. Research proposals should be requested only as an aid in deciding whether to conduct the research and/or which research firm to use. Similarly, proposals should be evaluated solely on their merit unless the other criteria (size and/or special capabilities of the research firm) are made known in advance. Proposals from one research firm should not be given to a second firm or an in-house research department for implementation.

Figure 5–4. Information to be Included in the Research Firm's Report

Every research project differs from all others. So will every research report. All reports should nonetheless contain specific reference to the following items:

1. The objectives of the study (including statement of hypotheses)
2. The name of the organization for which the study is made and the name of the organization that conducted it
3. Dates the survey was in the field and date of submission of final report
4. A copy of the full interview questionnaire, including all cards and visual aids, used in the interview; alternatively, exact question wording, sequence of questions, etc.
5. Description of the universe(s) studied
6. Description of the number and type sof people studied:
    a. Number of people (or other units)
    b. Means of their selection
    c. If sample, method of sample selection
    d. Adequacy of sample representation and size
    e. Percentage of original sample contacted (number and type of callbacks)
    f. Range of tolerance (sample error)
    g. Number of cases for category breakouts
    h. Weighting and estimating procedures used

Where trend data are being reported and the methodology or question wording has been changed, these changes sould be so noted.

On request—clients and other parties with legitimate interests may request and should expect to receive from the research firm the following:

a. Statistical and/or field methods of interview verification (and percentage of interviews verified)
b. Available data revalidation of interview techniques
c. Explanation of scoring or index number devices

Source: Paper developed by The Market Research Council's Ethics Committee. Reprinted with permission from Leo Bogart, ed., *Current Controversies in Marketing Research* (Rand McNally College Publishing Company, 1969), p. 156. Copyright © 1969 by Markham Publishing Company, Chicago. Reprinted by permission of Rand McNally College Publishing Company.

Disclosure of Proprietary Information or Techniques. Research firms often develop special techniques for dealing with certain types of problems. Examples are models for predicting the success of new products, models for allocating advertising expenditures among media, and simulation techniques for predicting the effects of changes in the mix variables. Research firms properly regard these techniques as being proprietary. The client should not make these techniques known to other research firms or appropriate them for its own use without the explicit consent of the developer.

Misrepresentation of Findings. Suppose the Honest and Ethical Research Firm is commissioned to do a study of analgesics by the manufacturer of

Brand A aspirin. In its report of the finding, the statement is made that "Brand A aspirin was reported to be the aspirin most preferred by two of three respondents using only aspirin as an analgesic for headaches." In its advertising on television to consumers, however, the firm makes the statement, "According to a study conducted by the Honest and Ethical Research Firm, two of three consumers preferred Brand A aspirin to all other products for treatment of headaches."

This is a clear distortion of the findings. It not only misleads the viewer but also is potentially damaging to the research firm. Other manufacturers of analgesics will recognize that this is not a true statement and may conclude that the research firm is guilty either of careless research or of dishonesty in reporting the results.

Corporate Espionage

Observation techniques are widely used to monitor shifts in competitors' prices, advertising, products, and the like. No ethical issue is involved in observing the public behavior of competitors. Corporate espionage is not concerned with this type of observation; instead it refers to observations of activities or products that the competitor is taking reasonable care to conceal from public view. Activities of this nature pose both ethical and legal questions. In the words of Judge Irving L. Goldberg of the U.S. Fifth Circuit Court of Appeals:

> Our devotion to free-wheeling industrial competition must not force us into accepting the law of the jungle as a standard of morality expected in our commercial relations. . . . One may use his competitor's secret process if he discovers it by his own independent research; but one may not avoid these labors by taking the process from the discoverer without his permission at a time when he is taking reasonable precautions to maintain its secrecy. ["The Great Game," 1970, p. 30]

Judge Goldberg was speaking in reference to the use of aerial photography in an attempt to discover the nature of a secret but unpatented production process during the construction of a new plant. Espionage techniques include activities such as electronic eavesdropping, bribing the competitor's employees, planting spies in a competitor's organization, sifting through garbage, eavesdropping at bars frequented by the competitor's employees, and hiring away the competitor's employees to learn of their future plans or secret processes.

The threat, real or imagined, of espionage by competitors has led many firms to install elaborate security systems. These systems may be internal or external. It is a sad comment that the industrial counterespionage business is apparently flourishing although it is not clear that espionage is a widespread practice (Furash 1959).

Techniques of corporate espionage have not been described in any detail in this chapter because we do not consider such activities to be a legitimate part of the business world, much less an acceptable part of the marketing research function. Many of these practices are illegal, and all are unethical. They are referred to here only to prevent the reader from naively thinking that they do not exist.

References

Bogart, L. 1962. "The Researcher's Dilemma." *Journal of Marketing* (January), p. 9.

Carlson, R.O. 1967. "The Issue of Privacy in Public Opinion Research." *Public Opinion Quarterly* (Spring), p. 5.

Crawford, C.M. 1970. "Attitudes of Marketing Executives towards Ethics in Marketing Research." *Journal of Marketing* (April), pp. 46–52.

Day, R.L. 1975. "A Comment on 'Ethics in Marketing Research,' " *Journal of Marketing Research* (May), pp. 232–233.

Diamond, S.A. 1982. "Market Research Latest Target in Ad Claims." *Advertising Age*, January 25, p. 52.

Dubinsky, A.J., and W. Rudelius. 1980. "Ethical Beliefs." In *Marketing in the 80's*, R.P. Bagozzi, et al., eds. Chicago: American Marketing Association, pp. 73–76.

Frey, C.J., and T.C. Kinnear. 1980. "Legal Constraints and Marketing Research." *Journal of Marketing Research* (August), pp. 295–302

Furash, E.E. 1959. "Industrial Espionage." *Harvard Business Review* (November–December), p. 6.

Gelb, B.D., and R.H. Brien. 1971. "Survival and Social Responsibility: Themes for Marketing Education and Management." *Journal of Marketing* (April), pp. 3–9.

Goldfield, E.D. 1977. "Two Studies Probe Public's Feelings on Being Surveyed." *Marketing News*, March 25, p. 6.

"The Great Game of Corporate Espionage." 1970. *Dun's Review* (October), p. 30.

Hawkins, D.I. 1979. "The Impact of Sponsor Identification and Direct Disclosure of Respondent Rights on the Quantity and Quality of Mail Survey Data." *Journal of Business* (October), pp. 557–590.

Hawkins, D.I., and A.B. Coconaugher. 1972. "Student Evaluations of the Ethics of Marketing Practices: The Role of Marketing Education." *Journal of Marketing* (April), pp. 61–64.

Hollander, S. 1974. "Ethics in Marketing Research." In *Handbook of Marketing Research*, R. Ferber, ed. New York: McGraw-Hill Book Co., pp. 1.107–1.127.

McMahon, T.F. 1968. "A Look at Marketing Ethics." *Atlanta Economic Review* (March), pp. 5–8.

Murphy, P.E., and G.R. Laczniak. 1981. "Marketing Ethics." In *Review of Marketing 1981*, B.M. Enis and K.J. Roering, eds. Chicago: American Marketing Association, pp. 251–266.

Shuptrine, F.K. 1979. "Evaluating the Ethics of Marketing Practices." In *1979 Educator's Conference Proceedings*, N. Beckwith et al., eds. Chicago: American Marketing Association, pp. 124–127.

Singer, E. 1978a. "Informed Consent: Consequences for Response Rate and Response Quality in Social Surveys." *American Sociological Review* (April), pp. 144–162.

——— . 1978b. "The Effect of Informed Consent Procedures on Respondents' Reactions to Surveys." *Journal of Consumer Research* (June), pp. 49–57.

Smith, J.G. 1979. "Should We Measure Involuntary Responses?" *Journal of Advertising Research* (October), pp. 35–39.

Tybout, A.M., and G. Zaltman. 1974. "Ethics in Marketing Research: Their Practical Relevance." *Journal of Marketing Research* (November), pp. 357–368.

——— . 1975. "A Reply to Comments on 'Ethics in Marketing Research: Their Practical Relevance,' " *Journal of Marketing Research* (May), pp. 234–237.

U.S. Executive Office of the President. Office of Science and Technology. 1967. *Privacy and Behavioral Research*. Washington, D.C.: U.S. Government Printing Office.

6
Ethics, Price Fixing, and the Management of Price Strategy

William J. Kehoe

P ricing is perhaps the most difficult area to examine from an ethical viewpoint of all the areas of marketing because of the complexity of the price variable. Pricing decisions are made at all levels of a distribution system. They are influenced by the profit goals of the firm and are constrained by federal and state laws. As Walton (1969, p. 209) observed, "perhaps no other area of managerial activity is more difficult to depict accurately, assess fairly and prescribe realistically in terms of morality than the domain of price."

It may be because of the complexity of price along with the greater appeal of ethical issues in other marketing areas that there is limited literature on the ethics of pricing. The available literature is found in business ethics books in sections on pricing, in articles dealing with sales force and buyer/seller issues (for example, Helfand 1977; Rudelius and Buchholz 1979; Dubinsky, Berkowitz, and Rudelius 1980; Dubinsky and Gwin 1981), in articles dealing with marketing management issues (Sturdivant and Cocanougher 1973; Ferrell and Weaver 1978), in articles dealing with price fixing (Lawyer 1963; Sonnenfeld and Lawrence 1978; Sonnenfeld 1981; Jacobs 1981; McClenahan 1981), in various review and theoretical articles on ethics (Bartel 1967; Trawick and Darden 1980; Murphy and Laczniak 1981; Kehoe 1982), and in a variety of articles dealing with codes of ethics.

Concept of Price

Price is a designation (usually monetary) used to facilitate exchange of a product or service at a particular time and place and to particular specifications. Theoretically, price is determined in a way that maximizes profit. More

Continuing support for this research in ethics from the McIntire School of Commerce, University of Virginia, is gratefully acknowledged as well as earlier support from the Center for Advanced Study and the Center for the Study of Applied Ethics at the University of Virginia.

realistically, pricing decisions are made on either a cost-plus basis, a target rate of return basis, a competition-oriented basis, or through analysis of the demand for the product/service.

Ethically, any price set by a firm should be either equal or proportional to the benefit received. The critical questions are, What are the benefits? How are they perceived by the consumer? For example, if a perceived benefit of a product is the status gained from the use of the product, does such a benefit justify charging a higher price for the product? If a product is defined in the larger sense as a bundle of want-satisfying qualities, the answer to the status/price question is different than if the product is more narrowly defined.

In a sense, a manager might use analysis by "proportionate reason" (Williams 1982) in considering the price/benefit question; that is, are there features of the action of charging a higher price, given some perceived benefit of the product, that justify the higher price as moral, even though the action may also have some form of wrong? For example, is it wrong to charge a price that yields extraordinary profit to the firm even if the market is willing to pay the price?

Concept of Profit

Most businesspeople would argue that business is entitled to profit so it can continue to exist in the long run. Profit is a reward to the organization for being successful in providing well-designed goods and/or services for the public, for risk taking, for efficient management, for effective marketing, and for being sensitive to the needs of its clients and other publics.

Profit is defined in economics as the excess of total revenue over total cost. Profit may also be defined as the return enjoyed by the organization on some balance sheet or income statement entry as the result of engaging in a successful exchange relationship. For example, the return on sales, the return on assets, the return on invested capital, and so on are used to describe the profit situation of a firm.

Both business and the public expect an organization to earn reasonable profit. Profit that appears too large, either in terms of its absolute magnitude or in terms of comparison with other firms, is considered by some people as unethical, especially if the profit has been preceded by prices that are perceived to be too high.

The petroleum industry is a case in point. Since about 1970, prices have increased dramatically. At the same time, petroleum companies are reporting record revenue and profit. The question becomes, is the profit reasonable or is it a windfall profit? Does the profit adequately reward the organization for risk taking and for effectiveness and efficiency in operations? When judged on the basis of return on invested capital, one might argue that there is a need for additional profit in the petroleum industry. Of course, such an argument must recognize the caveat that the industry is capital intensive.

It is not easy to judge the reasonableness of profit, and it is far more complex to decide whether the profit is ethical. A reasonable profit is one that rewards a firm for its contribution to the public good; allows a firm to reward shareholders competitively in its dividend payment; enables a firm's stock to compete in the equity market with other stocks and with bonds, certificates, and savings accounts; provides reinvestment for growth in the organization; and recognizes the degree of risk undertaken by a firm.

If a firm earns a reasonable profit using these criteria, is it also an ethical profit? Based on utilitarian ethical base (Bowie 1982, p. 21), the argument could be advanced that a reasonable profit enables a firm to continue to produce goods and services for the benefit of society; that is, the greater good of society is being satisfied by a firm's having a reasonable profit.

Even though the greater good of society may be served by reasonable profit, one cannot conclude the profit is ethical solely on a utilitarian ethical base. Other important questions (Velasquez 1982, p. 18) must be brought to the analysis. Was society in any way injured in making the profit? Injury could occur from actions by the firm such as deceptive advertising, pollution, price fixing, fraud, concealed product defects, and so on. Were the employees of the organization adequately and fairly paid for their work in producing the product? Were the poor and disadvantaged afforded the opportunity of the product, or were they defined as a market segment of low interest to the firm? These and other questions must be addressed when judging whether a reasonable profit is also an ethical profit.

Ethical Issues in Pricing

Identifying the Issues

There is an expansive realm of ethical issues in pricing. Issues may be raised at all levels of the distribution channel, across different market structures and competitive situations, and across industry types. Murphy and Laczniak (1981) have identified the following ethical issues in pricing:

1. determining a fair price that meets corporate objectives while not taking advantage of consumers;
2. altering the quality and/or quantity of merchandise without changing the price;
3. practicing price discrimination with smaller accounts;
4. using multiple pricing deals at the retail level;
5. excessively marking up products that are given as premiums;
6. using lower quality merchandise for end-of-month sales;

7. adding high markups to products sold by a franchisor to a franchisee;
8. engaging in price fixing.

Other ethical issues, identified by Dubinsky, Berkowitz, and Rudelius (1980) and Dubinsky and Gwin (1981), include:

9. having less competitive prices or terms of sale for those buyers who use a firm as their only supplier;
10. providing gifts, prizes, or purchase volume incentive bonuses to some customers and not to others;
11. obtaining information on a competitor's price quotation in order to re-quote or rebid;
12. using a firm's economic power to force premium prices on a buyer;
13. using reciprocity practices.

Beyond these issues, other pricing activities of questionable ethics identified in this research include:

14. the situation of a manufacturer printing a suggested retail price (list price) on a product or its package with the knowledge the retailer does not intend to sell at the suggested retail price but intends to mark over the price to give the impression the item has been marked down—the list price should be the price at which an item is usually and customarily sold, according to the FTC in a case examining the meaning of list (Beauchamp and Bowie 1979, p. 447);
15. the practice of pricing branded products higher than generic products—Benson (1982, p. 110) notes that "no ethic has been determined" regarding the pricing practices of branded versus generic products;
16. using special price codes (as in automobile dealerships with used cars) so that the consumer cannot easily compare prices;
17. failing to put the price on the product or to post it at the point of purchase, as is often done in the case of a retailer's use of UPCs;
18. bribery of purchasers to cause them to accept higher prices on items in the purchase order;
19. failure of retailers to pass on to consumers discounts to which they are entitled;
20. the practice of psychological pricing (e.g. intending that the consumer will perceive $299 as "about $200").

Choosing an Issue

A single issue, price fixing, is chosen for further analysis. This choice was made because the ethics and legality of price fixing have an extensive literature; price fixing is not only one of the oldest but also a contemporary ethical issue in pricing; and the conclusions, recommendations, and implications taken from an analysis of the ethical issues in price fixing may be generalized to other pricing situations.

Price Fixing

Price fixing is an illegal activity. It is forbidden by antitrust legislation. Antitrust law has been described by Austin (1961) as a set of laws that forms an externally imposed code of conduct and ethics that stipulate:

1. Business firms must not conspire to monopolize a market.
2. Business firms must not conspire to allocate shares of a market among themselves.
3. Business firms should not conspire to agree jointly as to the prices at which products will be sold.

The Sherman Antitrust Act of 1890, the Clayton Act of 1914, the Federal Trade Commission Act of 1914, and the Robinson-Putman Act of 1936 comprise what is commonly referred to as antitrust law.

Price fixing is any practice in which a firm conspires with other firms to set minimum or maximum prices, set production quotas, rig bids, eliminate discounts, limit price advertising, or pressure distributors to sell at suggested retail prices (so-called vertical price fixing) (Jacobs 1981). Lawyer (1963) explained how to conspire to fix prices but admonished that a firm may not benefit by conspiring even if it does not get caught.

The penalty for being convicted of price fixing is severe. A convicted firm can be required to pay three times the total overcharges made by all price fixers in a market (McClenahan 1981). Under the proposed Antitrust Equal Enforcement Act, each company would have its liability for damages limited to the percentage of total industry sales it realized during the conspiracy. As an example, presently, a major manufacturer convicted of price fixing is liable for $700 million in damages, while under the proposed legislation, the damages would be reduced—that is, limited—to $53 million ("Trying to Put . . ." 1982, pp. 54 and 56).

Examples of price fixing activities have been reported in the literature. The best known examples are from the electrical manufacturing and folding carton industries. These are presented here and their similarities are noted to suggest guidelines for operating ethically.

Electrical Manufacturers' Case

In the electrical manufacturers' case, price was decentralized. This meant that operating managers were allowed to determine price and that significant pressure was applied on the managers to make profit goals. This, combined with the fact that collusion was perceived to be condoned by management, led to a conspiracy to fix prices in the industry.

In price fixing litigation in 1961, General Electric, Westinghouse, and other manufacturers were charged with conspiracy. The electrical manufacturing industry is an oligopoly market. In an oligopoly, there are few sellers, a substantial share of the market is controlled by a small number of the firms, and the firms are affected by each other's pricing practices, especially if the products are undifferentiated. There is an interdependence in pricing in an oligopoly because the number of firms is so few that any firm immediately notices and is affected by the pricing decisions of a competitor (Bell 1964). An oligopoly, therefore, tends to establish price uniformity, particularly in an undifferentiated oligopoly. This is accomplished by each firm carefully monitoring the pricing actions of competitors and maintaining similar prices or by price leadership, collusion, or conspiracy.

Folding Carton Industry Case

The folding carton industry is significantly different from the electrical manufacturing industry; it is not an oligopoly. At the time of its price fixing litigation in mid-1970, the industry had over 450 companies, with the largest controlling under 10 percent of the market. Its products were undifferentiated and there was a job order nature to the business in which each job was costed and priced individually. This forced the pricing decision and authority lower in the organization and effectively decentralized the decision.

Management in the folding carton industry appraised individual performance on the basis of profit and volume. The market was crowded, there was widespread participation by employees in trade associations, and the corporate legal staffs were reactive and allowed managers to engage in questionable price practices.

Synthesis

The following company-level similarities identified by Sonnenfeld and Lawrence (1978) in these two case examples suggest company situations where there may be pressure to price in an unethical fashion:

1. undifferentiated products;
2. decentralized pricing;
3. pressure to achieve profit goals;
4. collusion perceived to be condoned by top management;
5. reactive versus anticipatory corporate legal staffs;
6. general ethical rules as opposed to specific ethical rules;
7. no ethical compliance procedures or ethical audits.

Reasons for Unethical Pricing Behavior

Price fixing is illegal. However, even in the absence of law, the expectation would be that ethics would prevent price fixing. In fact, it did not and has not.

When Sonnenfeld (1981) interviewed senior executives and divisional managers from four of the ten largest producers in the folding carton industry, he received role-biased responses to the question, why does your company have difficulty avoiding price fixing? The senior executives attributed price fixing to dispositional factors such as individual uncontrollable variations in human morals, obedience, and intelligence. They felt violators should be punished as a deterrence to others and recommended employee selection surveillance, reward tightening, and policy clarification as ways to prevent price fixing in the future. The divisional managers blamed price fixing on situational factors like declining demand and treated violators as conscientious people who happened to be caught.

A probable reason why senior executives blamed the individual for price fixing while divisional managers blamed the situation is that the divisional managers were closer to both the individual and the situation than the senior executives. Beyond these proximate reasons of individual and situation, there are other reasons for unethical behavior. A study sponsored by the Business Roundtable (Steckmest 1982, pp. 74–75), suggested that unethical corporate behavior is caused by at least six organizational reasons:

Corporate objectives and review procedures that overemphasize the profit criterion. If profit goals are overemphasized, line managers may perceive that profit should be placed above ethical considerations. In both case examples discussed earlier, pressure to achieve profit goals contributed to price fixing behavior. As Clasen (1967, p. 82) observed, when the choice is between profit margins and ethics at the line management level, profit margins are often chosen.

Ethical standards without a concomitant control system. If the ethical standard is, for example, never to lower product quality without also reviewing the necessity of a price adjustment, this standard will become ineffective if it is not monitored by management, particularly if line management is profit oriented. This is because a single job objective is being emphasized.

Allowing the law to be a surrogate for corporate ethics. This should never be permitted to occur. Rather, as stated in the Caterpillar Tractor Company's Code of Worldwide Business Conduct, "the law is a floor. Ethical business conduct should normally exist at a level well above the minimum required by law" (Walton 1977, p. 82). In situations where the law is vague or permissive, the highest integrity should be expected.

Ambiguous corporate policies. If policy is unclear as to the ethical conduct that is expected in making a pricing decision, the employee may be unsure whether the policy is to be observed. In the absence of the requirements of law in a particular pricing practice, management should determine if its policy specifically indicates the expected behavior on the part of the employee and the outcome if the behavior is not performed. For example, the policy of the IBM Corporation is clearly never to discuss price with competitors. If such a discussion ever occurs, the IBM policy is that the representative "should leave in a manner that will be noticed and remembered by others at the meeting" (Rudelius and Buchholz 1979, p. 11).

Misreading public concern about corporate ethics. The public has become increasingly concerned about business ethics. In a major ethical incident (for example, bribery by a large corporation), the public becomes sensitive about the ethical conduct of all business firms. In such a situation, price leadership actions, for example, while legal, may be questioned on the basis of ethics.

Amoral decision making. When profit is the criterion in the pricing decision, ethical implications of the decision and its impact on people are often overlooked. For example, the situation of establishing higher prices in a captive market, like a lower income neighborhood where people shop at the neighborhood retail outlet, is a situation of being more concerned about profit and less concerned about people, except to the extent that people affect profit projections.

These six organizational reasons, together with the proximate reasons of individual disposition and situation, give insight to reasons for questionable ethics in pricing. These reasons, in turn, are useful in formulating guidelines for improving pricing ethics.

Areas for Research

As mentioned earlier, the paucity of research on pricing ethics provides opportunity for future research of the theoretical, empirical, and applied (case research) natures. Potential research questions include the following:

What are the ethical beliefs of managers with pricing authority versus those without pricing authority? Does being assigned profit-and-loss responsibility change a manager's ethical beliefs? Replication of the Ferrell and Weaver (1978) research using these questions would be interesting and useful.

Does ethical pricing enhance revenue and profit? What are the ethical implications of centralized versus decentralized pricing?

How are ethical concepts and theories internalized, personalized, and used by marketing representatives in the pricing decision using both direct and indirect research measures?

What are the types and frequencies of ethical violations in pricing in product versus services marketing? As services marketing involves pricing and selling an intangible, are service marketers less ethical than product marketers in making pricing decisions?

What is the relationship of market structure (pure competition, monopoly, monopolistic competition, oligopoly) to ethics in pricing?

What is the relationship between a sales representative's performance and success and his or her ethical stance? Are successful representatives more ethical in pricing than unsuccessful representatives?

What is the impact of the electronic approaches to pricing (for example, Universal Product Codes) on consumers' perceptions of ethics in pricing? What steps can management take to increase consumer confidence in the ethics of the electronic approaches to pricing?

What is the impact of codes of ethics on the competitive nature of a market? What is the impact of codes of ethics on pricing decisions?

Management Guidelines

Organizations should take pragmatic steps to improve ethical practice in pricing. Recommended here are steps involving four areas: the employee, the market situation, the corporation, and the consumer.

The Employee

Education of the employee in the concept of ethics is critical to improving ethical practice in pricing. The educational program, in its content and pedagogy, should seek to increase the employee's sensitivity toward the ethical dimension of the pricing decision, to imbue an understanding of ethical theory and concepts to enable the employee to analyze ethical issues in the pricing decision, to develop a capacity for resolution of ethical issues, and to enable the employee to recognize when to seek professional help from management. The corporate position and its code of ethics should be promulgated and examples of likely ethical situations and dilemmas presented and discussed during the educational program. Both positive and negative outcomes should be explored.

Finally, the educational program should cause questions of ethics to be routinely reported to and discussed with management. This is the obverse of a monitoring system and will enhance compliance.

The Market Situation

Guidelines for pricing ethics might be approached by analyzing pricing from two market viewpoints. At one extreme, the pricing decision is decentralized, the product is homogeneous, and the field sales representative has a wide range of pricing authority. At the other extreme, pricing is highly centralized, the product is differentiated, the price is administered by marketing management, and the field sales representative has little authority to deviate from the established price. In the former, ethics in pricing is addressed at the field sales level, while in the latter, it is addressed at the management level.

The more decentralized the pricing decision, the greater is the number of individuals who will have some degree of pricing authority. If the market is highly competitive, prices are quoted on a job basis, and the product is differentiated, it behooves management to be especially concerned that employees remain ethical and legal in pricing. In such a situation, ethics must be institutionalized in the firm, especially in the marketing area.

The Corporation

Purcell (1982) has recommended institutionalizing ethics in the corporation by placing an ethics committee on the board of directors; by establishing, promulgating, and using a corporate code of ethics; and by including ethics modules and courses in management training programs. Similarly, ethics must be institutionalized in the marketing area of the corporation. This may be accomplished by:

1. including a session on ethics at the annual sales meeting;
2. building an ethics module into the orientation program of new employees;
3. including discussion of ethics in the annual review meeting with marketing employees (the purpose here is to gain insight into individual dispositional factors that might influence pricing ethics);
4. briefly discussing ethics on a quarterly basis in employee newsletters;
5. requiring sales representatives to certify that they have not knowingly violated laws or ethical policy in securing any purchase order they submit to the firm;
6. circulating articles on ethics to the sales representatives;
7. inviting consultants and/or educators to conduct regular seminars on ethics.

The Consumer

One of the most important things a firm can do to improve ethics in pricing is to recognize that the consumer is an equal partner with the firm in the exchange relationship. The consumer brings needs and expectations to the exchange, is entitled to be fairly treated in the pricing process, and has certain rights that should be respected by the firm. What follows is a statement of consumer rights in pricing:

> A consumer is entitled to receive fair value for the money spent to purchase a product or service. He or she has the right to expect that the price was realistically and analytically arrived at by the firm and was calculated to give the firm a reasonable profit (defined earlier in this chapter). The price should be fully disclosed by being stated in advertisements for the product or service, posted at the point of sale, and placed on the product (although the use of UPCs confounds this requirement). The price on the product should be the price at which the seller is willing to enter an exchange. It should not be artificially high so it causes the buyer to believe he or she has received a bargain when the price is lowered in negotiation to its intended level. When the product is changed in quality or quantity, the customer is entitled to receive a proportional change in price. Price changes should be promptly announced and completely implemented. Questions concerning price should be honestly answered. Customers are always entitled to fair and equal pricing treatment in the marketplace.

These are several advantages to a firm in adopting the statement of consumer rights in pricing. Internally, the statement becomes a code of pricing ethics that sensitizes employees to the necessity of being ethical in pricing and in other marketing activities. Externally, the statement communicates to potential clients that the firm is oriented toward being ethical in pricing.

Conclusion

In the beginning of this chapter, Walton's (1969) observation on the difficulty in examining ethical issues in pricing was noted. That observation still stands. Price is a complex marketing variable, and it is difficult to assess ethically.

While ethics in pricing is difficult to assess, certain conclusions may be drawn that are of value to management. A firm may have difficulty with ethics in pricing when:

1. the market is at overcapacity or characterized as an oligopoly;
2. products are undifferentiated;
3. pricing is on an individual job basis;

4. profit is the primary evaluative criterion;
5. top management is perceived not to be concerned about pricing ethics;
6. employees have regular and frequent opportunities to meet with competitors;
7. ethical rules and compliance procedures are lax.

If one or several of these characteristics is present, management must be concerned with ethics in pricing. To ensure ethical practices in pricing, management should audit pricing policy and practice, institutionalize a concern for ethics in pricing, and establish a means for reviewing the pricing activity. In situations where the characteristics listed here are not present, competition should not be considered a sufficient guarantee of ethical pricing; rather, management must remain vigilant and monitor pricing decisions. These actions will ensure ethics in pricing.

Beyond ethics in pricing, management and employees should aspire to be ethical in all aspects of work. Pope John Paul II, in his *Encyclical Laborem Exercens (On Human Work)* (1981, p. 86), asks that employees be ethical in all aspects of work. The encyclical states "that man, created in the image of God, shares by his work in the activity of the Creator and that, within the limits of his own human capabilities, man in a sense continues to develop that activity, and perfects it as he advances further and further in the discovery of the resources and values contained in the whole creation." In the presence of this profound concept of work, is it too much to ask that managers be ethical in the work of pricing?

References

Austin, Robert W. 1961. "A Code of Conduct for Executives." *Harvard Business Review* 39 (September–October), pp. 53–61.

Bartels, Robert. 1967. "A Model for Ethics in Marketing." *Journal of Marketing* 31 (January), pp. 20–26.

Beauchamp, Tom L., and N.E. Bowie. 1979. *Ethical Theory and Business*. Englewood Cliffs, N.J.: Prentice-Hall, Inc.

Bell, Martin L. 1964. "Ethics in Oligopoly Pricing Practices." In *Ethics and Standards in American Business*, J.W. Towle, ed. Boston: Houghton Mifflin Company, pp. 196–209.

Benson, George. 1982. *Business Ethics in America*. Lexington, Mass.: D.C. Heath and Company, Lexington Books.

Bowie, Norman. 1982. *Business Ethics*. Englewood Cliffs, N.J.: Prentice-Hall, Inc.

Clasen, Earl A. 1967. "Marketing Ethics and the Consumer." *Harvard Business Review* 45 (January–February), pp. 79–86.

Dubinsky, Alan J., and John M. Gwin. 1981. "Business Ethics: Buyers and Sellers." *Journal of Purchasing and Materials Management* (Winter), pp. 9–16.

Dubinsky, Alan J., E.N. Berkowitz, and W. Rudelius. 1980. "Ethical Problems of Field Sales Personnel." *MSU Business Topics* (Summer), pp. 11–16.

Ferrell, O.C., and K.M. Weaver. 1978. "Ethical Beliefs of Marketing Managers." *Journal of Marketing* 42 (July), pp. 69–73.

Helfand, T. 1977. "Setting Conduct Code for Marketers." *Industrial Marketing* (February), p. 9.

Jacobs, Bruce A. 1981. "Price Fixing: Is It Worth the Risk?" *Industry Week* 210 (August 24, 1981), pp. 43–48.

John Paul II. 1981. *Encyclical Laborem Exercens.* Rome, St. Paul Press Edition (September 14).

Kehoe, William J. 1982. "Marketing Ethics: Theory and Pedagogy." In *Developments in Marketing Science, vol. 5,* V. Kothari, ed. Nacogdoches, Texas: Academy of Marketing Sciences, pp. 261–264.

Lawyer, John Q. 1963. "How to Conspire to Fix Prices." *Harvard Business Review* 41 (March–April), pp. 95–103.

McClenahan, John. 1981. "Business Fights to Alter Price Fixing Law." *Industry Week* 211 (October 5), pp. 17–18.

Murphy, Patrick E., and Gene R. Laczniak. 1981. "Marketing Ethics: A Review with Implications for Managers, Educators and Researchers." In *Review of Marketing 1981,* Ben M. Enis and Kenneth J. Roering, eds. Chicago: American Marketing Association, pp. 251–266.

Purcell, Theodore V., S.J. 1982. "The Ethics of Corporate Governance." *Review of Social Economy* 40 (December), pp. 360–370.

Rudelius, William, and R.A. Buchholz. 1979. "Ethical Problems of Purchasing Managers." *Harvard Business Review* 57 (March–April), pp. 8, 12, and 14.

Sonnenfeld, Jeffrey. 1981. "Executive Apologies for Price Fixing: Role Biased Perceptions of Causality." *Academy of Management Journal* 24 (March), pp. 192–198.

Sonnenfeld, Jeffrey, and P.R. Lawrence. 1978. "Why Do Companies Succumb to Price Fixing?" *Harvard Business Review* 56 (July–August), pp. 145–157.

Steckmest, Francis W. 1982. *Corporate Performance: The Key to Public Trust.* New York: McGraw-Hill Book Company.

Sturdivant, Frederick D., and A.B. Cocanougher. 1973. "What Are Ethical Marketing Practices?" *Harvard Business Review* 51 (November–December), pp. 10–11 and 176.

Trawick, Fred, and W.R. Darden. 1980. "Marketers' Perceptions of Ethical Standards in the Marketing Profession: Educators and Practitioners." *Review of Business and Economic Research* 16 (Fall), pp. 1–17.

"Trying to Put a Ceiling on Price Fixers' Liability." 1982. *Business Week,* (May 24), pp. 54 and 56.

Velasquez, M.G. 1982. *Business Ethics.* Englewood Cliffs, N.J.: Prentice-Hall, Inc.

Walton, Clarence C. 1969. *Ethos and the Executive.* Englewood Cliffs, N.J.: Prentice-Hall, Inc.

———. 1977. *Ethics of Corporate Conduct.* Englewood Cliffs, N.J.: Prentice-Hall, Inc.

Williams, Oliver F. 1982. "Business Ethics: A Trojan Horse." *California Management Review* 24 (Summer), pp. 14–24.

7
Ethical Issues in Multinational Marketing

David J. Fritzsche

Business has been accused of unethical practices in international dealings since international trade began. Marketing activities have been central to international trade and thus have been the focus of much of the criticism concerning unethical behavior. Public policymakers have attempted to alter the behavior of firms engaged in foreign trade from time to time through the public policy process, with the most recent attempt being the passage of the Foreign Corrupt Practices Act of 1977. However, it is difficult to legislate ethics.

The focus of this chapter is the ethical aspects of marketing activities in the international arena. Before proceeding, let us set the stage by examining some of these practices. Marketing has been criticized for offering harmful products to underdeveloped countries. These products are of two types: products that are banned in the United States and products that are unsuitable for use in developing countries. An example of a product that is banned in the United States but sold abroad is DDT. While banned in this country in 1972 (Council on Environmental Quality 1973), DDT is still being sold to Third World countries for use in controlling malaria. An example of a product that is claimed to be unsuitable for use in underdeveloped countries is infant formula that is substituted for mother's milk. Critics claim that the milk substituted is misused by the populace of the countries because of ignorance and poverty. As a result, thousands of children suffer from malnutrition and/or starvation (Post 1978).

Marketing has also been criticized for promoting its products through bribes and payoffs. One of the more notable cases involved Lockheed Aircraft Corporation's payment to former Japanese Prime Minister Tanaka to assist in the sale of Lockheed aircraft. In addition, Prince Bernhard of the Netherlands was accused of accepting money from Lockheed in connection with the sale of F-104 Starfighter jets. Lockheed admitted making payments to officials in at least fifteen countries including Greece, Italy, Nigeria, Turkey, and South Africa ("Payoffs" 1976).

In the area of distribution, firms have been accused of payoffs used to buy their way into the country's distribution network or production facilities.

Del Monte Corporation paid nearly $500,000 to a so-called business consultant in Guatemala to assist in the purchase of a banana plantation. The government had refused their request for 18 months. Once the company paid the consultant, the government reversed its decision and the deal was approved ("Fruitful Association" 1975).

In the area of pricing, numerous companies have been charged with dumping their products in other countries at a price below production costs. Most of the criticism has been against European and Japanese companies for dumping products (like steel) in the United States. However, the Celanese Corporation, Union Carbide Corporation, and Gantrade Corporation were found guilty of dumping vinyl acetate monomer on the Common Market ("Common Market" 1981).

Differences in Ethical Views

A number of these practices are legal in some countries. *Baksheesh* (lubrication payment) is often the accepted manner of doing business in the Middle and Far East. However, one must be careful not to confuse ethics with the law.

The ethical practices of business tend to vary from country to country. In one study (Fritzsche and Becker 1984), marketers in the United States, Germany, and France were asked to evaluate the ethical standards in marketing of the following countries: the United Kingdom, France, Germany, Greece, India, Israel, Italy, Japan, Mexico, and the United States. Responses were obtained using a mail survey with the instrument translated into French and German. A total of 72 French, 70 German, and 124 American marketers responded to the survey.

The results, shown in table 7–1, reveal a significant variation in the perceptions of the various countries. The data were derived by asking the respondents to rank each of the ten countries in terms of that country's ethical standards. The data shown are the median values of the ranked data from marketers in the three countries. Germany is perceived to be the most ethical country by marketers from all three of the countries. Germany was followed by the United Kingdom and then the United States and France. Mexico was ranked lowest, with India and Italy not far behind. The data were subjected to a Kruskal-Wallis one-way analysis of variance technique to determine whether the rankings of each country provided by the marketers from the three countries were significantly different.

The French standards were perceived to be lower by the German and American respondents than by the French. Both the Germans and the Americans ranked Greece higher than it was ranked by the French. Conversely, the French ranked Italy and Mexico higher than the Germans and the Americans ranked the two countries. The greatest difference appeared in the U.S. ranking:

Table 7–1
Perceptions of Ethical Standards in Marketing Provided by French, German, and U.S. Marketers

Country Ranked	Respondents			
	French Median	German Median	U.S. Median	Average Median
United Kingdom	3	3	3	3
France	3	5	5	4[a]
Germany	2	2	2	2
Greece	8	7	7	7[a]
India	8	9	8	8
Israel	6	7	6	6
Italy	7	8	8	8[a]
Japan	5	5	4	5
Mexico	8	9	9	9[a]
United States	3	7	1	4[a]

Note: The data were obtained from respondent's rankings of the countries, with 1 representing the most ethical.
[a]Significance at the .05 level.

The American respondents ranked the U.S. standards as highest. The French ranked them lower, and the Germans ranked the United States significantly lower at seven. This indicates an extreme difference in perceptions toward the United States among marketers in the three countries.

Certainly some nationalism is evidenced among the marketers who participated in the study. However, other factors were at work, as evidenced by the French ranking the Germans as high as the Germans ranked themselves. If these data are representative of the actual ethical practices being followed, one can hypothesize that the level of ethical behavior tends to increase with the level of economic development of the country. Whether this increase is caused by developments in the legal system of the country or by society's expectations and the needs of the participants is unknown.

One must remember that the respondents in the study were from highly developed countries. Whether these relationships would hold if the evaluation were made by marketers from underdeveloped countries is open to question.

Ethical Standards

To evaluate the ethical dimensions of a business decision, one must possess some type of a yardstick against which to measure the ethical component of he decision. Unfortunately, not one but three yardsticks are commonly used to evaluate the ethical component of a decision. These yardsticks, or ethical standards, are commonly known as the *utilitarian principle*, the *rights principle*, and the *justice principle*. Each of these standards has its strengths and weaknesses that are well documented (Velasquez 1982). Due to time and space limitations, we discuss only the basic standards and not the pros and cons.

The utilitarian principle is summarized by Velasquez as follows:

> An action is right from an ethical point of view if and only if the sum total of utilities produced by that act is greater than the sum total of utilities produced by any other act the agent could have performed in its place. [1982, p. 47].

Two conditions are always considered unethical under the utilitarian standard. First, it is unethical to select an act that leads to an inefficient use of resources. Second, it is unethical to engage in an act that leads to personal gain at the expense of society.

The rights principle focuses on the individual rather than on society. Moral rights are not synonymous with legal rights; that is, a right may be moral and not legal, or a right may be legal and not moral. Moral rights are normally perceived as universal; that is, people are entitled to the rights simply by being human. A moral principle (which Kant calls the *categorical imperative*) provides a foundation for moral rights:

> An action is morally right for a person in a certain situation if and only if the person's reason for carrying out the action is a reason that he or she would be willing to have every person act on, in any similar situation. [Velasquez 1982, p. 66]

The rights principle discussed here is based on Kant's categorical imperative, which incorporates two criteria for judging the moral right and wrong of an action. The first criterion is "universalizability"; that is, the person's reasons for acting must be reasons that everyone could act on at least in principle. The second criterion is "reversibility"; that is, the person's reasons for acting must be reasons that he or she would be willing to have all others use, even as a basis of how they treat him or her (Velasquez 1982).

The justice principle is usually divided into three categories. Distributive justice, the category most directly related to the economic system, is concerned with the distribution of society's benefits and burdens. This principle may be summarized as follows:

> Individuals who are similar in all respects relevant to the kind of treatment in question should be given similar benefits and burdens, even if they are dissimilar in other respects; and individuals who are dissimilar in a relevant respect ought to be treated dissimilarly, in proportion to their dissimilarity.

Basically the principle holds that equals should be treated equally and that unequals should be treated unequally. Retributive justice, the second category, deals with blaming and punishing persons for doing wrong. It must first be ascertained that the individual committed the act. The person must have committed the act out of free choice and with knowledge of the consequences. Finally, the punishment must be consistent with and proportional to the wrongdoing. Compensatory justice, the third part of the justice principle, is concerned with compensation for the wronged individual. The compensation should be provided with the intent of restoring the injured party to his or her original position.

These three standards do not always lead to the same conclusions. It is not unusual for the application of the standards to lead to different conclusions, depending on the standard used. The decision maker must then decide which standard takes precedence.

Multinational Issues

Let us examine specific ethical problems in a multinational setting by applying the preceding ethical standards to a series of marketing activities. The problems are examined by the type of marketing issue they represent.

Product

> The drug Depo-Provera, manufactured by the Upjohn Corporation, is being sold to the Malaysian government for use in its birth control program. The Food and Drug Administration (FDA) has refused to license the drug in the United States because it has been shown to cause menstrual difficulties and has been linked with heart cancer in animals ("Watchdogs Abroad" 1980). Is Upjohn acting in an ethical manner in selling Depo-Provera to Malaysia?

In examining the issue from the utilitarian perspective, one must first look at the benefits derived from the drug. In this case, the benefits consist of the value derived from controlling the growth of the population in the country. The costs involved to society include the complications experienced by women in their menstrual cycle plus the loss of life that may result from the cancer. One is likely to conclude that alternative methods of birth control that have less risk are available and, thus, from the utilitarian perspective, that it is unethical to market Depo-Provera for this purpose.

Utilizing the rights and standards, one would expect that the reversibility criterion is being violated. Given that there are safer alternative methods of birth control, the people at Upjohn are likely to object to Depo-Provera for their personal use. The rights of the individuals receiving the injections are violated by the fact that they would not likely have consented to the injection given prior knowledge of the possible detrimental consequences of using the drug. They are subjected to risks without their knowledge and thus are not free to choose to have the injection.

The justice principle does not really come into play in this case. It would be appropriate to call for compensation after harm from the drug has occurred. However, prior to this time, there are no benefits or compensation to be allocated.

Based on this analysis, one must judge the marketing of Depo-Provera to be an unethical act given the knowledge of the harmful side effects created by the drug. A number of other chemicals that are banned in the United States but marketed abroad would be subjected to the same type of analysis. Included are the pesticides dieldrin, aldrin, heptachlor, and chlordane. It is entirely possible that several of these pesticides provide sufficient benefits to be justified on an ethical basis even though they have been banned by the Environmental Protection Agency.

Price

While the United States has accused a number of foreign companies of dumping their products on the U.S. market, there have also been instances where U.S. companies have been charged with dumping products on foreign markets. One of these is the European Common Market's finding that U.S.-produced styrene monomer was dumped on the European market at 26 percent below the quoted price in the United States ("Common Market" 1981). Is this a case of an unethical act by U.S. firms?

The societal benefits derived from this action, using the utilitarian principle, would consist of the lower cost product provided to the people in European countries plus the additional profits realized by the U.S. companies through the sale of the additional monomer. The social costs would consist of the damage done to the European companies, thus creating long-run social costs. There is also the unanswered question of whether the U.S. companies that did the dumping had other alternatives that would have yielded a greater benefit to society. Without having intimate knowledge of those costs and benefits, it is impossible to conclude whether this was an unethical act using the utilitarian criterion.

Dumping certainly violates the reversibility criterion of the rights standard. Companies doing the dumping would not agree to accept dumping from their foreign competitors. Thus, from a rights perspective, the dumping is unethical.

Dumping also violates the justice principle in that equals are not being treated as equals. The European firms are faced with meeting competition that is not covering its costs in foreign sales. The fixed costs are being covered by domestic sales, with foreign sales priced to cover only variable costs. Thus, the U.S. competition has an advantage that is not available to the European producers. It is a question of fairness.

The dumping action must also be judged unethical. It violates both the rights and the justice principles and possibly the utilitarian standard, although this is not certain.

Promotion

The Sam P. Wallace Company, a specialty construction company, paid the chairman of the Trinidad and Tobago Racing Commission 5 percent of the project cost to obtain the contract to build the grandstand and buildings for a new luxury horse racing track ("Robert Buckner" 1983). The chairman of the racing commission requested the payment to ease the project along. This, of course, is a bribe, which is illegal under the Foreign Corrupt Practices Act of 1977. Was the bribe unethical?

The utilitarian standard would say that the bribe was unethical because the construction could have been accomplished through the normal bidding process that, in theory at least, results in an efficient utilization of resources. The bribe may likely result in an inefficient utilization of resources in that a higher cost operator may get the contract. This is all the more likely given that the payoff is a percentage of the contract. The payoff also contributes to the cost of the project, with no increase in benefits. Thus, the racing commission chairman is benefiting at the expense of society, and this is clearly unethical.

The universalization criterion of the rights principle appears to be violated since one could not condone everyone paying a bribe to get business. This would lead to a world where bribing was a way of life and where only the rich could succeed.

The distributive aspect of the justice principle is violated by the bribe because the chairman of the racing commission is receiving more benefits than his equals. This unequal distribution among equals is the result of pressure applied in a situation of privilege that results in benefits not accorded to those who did not apply the pressure.

The bribe is thus judged to be unethical under all three ethical principles. It is not only unethical but also illegal. There is no redeeming value to a bribe.

Distribution

Continental Grain Corporation was charged with and pleaded guilty to shortweighing grain in overseas shipments. The scales used by the company to weigh corn, sorghum, and soybeans had been set to weigh 0.05 percent more than the actual weight ("Grain Concern" 1976). This results in a substantial amount of weight in a ship loaded with grain being charged to a country as phantom freight. This is clearly an illegal practice. One suspects that it is also unethical.

From a utilitarian perspective, the practice of shortweighing clearly is unethical. It is a classic example of private gain at society's expense. In terms of rights, the reversibility criterion is definitely violated. Continental would not agree to pay for items it did not receive. The foreign country did not freely choose to pay for the additional grain that it did not receive. Certainly, Continental would not advocate making this practice universal; to do so would destroy our system of weights and measures.

The justice principle is also violated because equals are not treated as equals. If a foreign company purchases grain from another country, it assumes it will get the grain for which it pays. However, it is shorted when buying from Continental. All three principles are violated by this practice of shortweighing. It has no redeeming merit.

We have reviewed the ethical principles that should be considered when evaluating the ethical aspects of a marketing decision. We have also applied these principles to real world business situations. It is time to formalize this process in terms of a model that can be used by managers in their decision process.

A Model for Ethical Decision Making

Figure 7–1 shows a model that can be used to guide the decision maker in the ethical aspects of making a decision. The model is a modification of one pro-

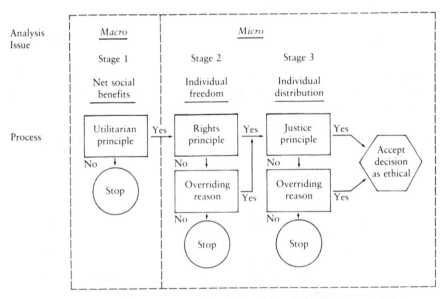

Figure 7–1. Ethical Decision Model

posed by Cavanaugh, Moberg, and Velasquez (1981). The model has been divided into two parts, the first being macro (dealing with the utilitarian benefits to society) and the second being micro (dealing with individuals). The model is discussed from the perspective of Fox Importers, a fictitious firm that is deciding whether it wants to participate in a so-called gray market for cameras. This would involve purchasing foreign cameras on the overseas market at prices below those charged to manufacturer-approved U.S. dealers. The cameras would then be sold to retailers at a favorable price that is likely to be lower than that available from the manufacturer-approved dealers.

The macro portion of the model serves as the screening device for the micro portion of the model. The action in question is analyzed from the standpoint of the net social benefits (NSB) provided society. If it appears that the action will provide NSB at least as great as any alternative action, the action is considered ethical from a utilitarian perspective. This is a necessary but insufficient condition for judging an act ethical. If the action does not satisfy the utilitarian standard, it is dropped from consideration.

Fox Importers must consider the situations of the consumers purchasing cameras, the camera manufacturers, the manufacturer-approved dealers, and their own economic welfare when evaluating the NSB of entering the gray market. The camera manufacturers are not likely to be affected by the action since they will sell the cameras regardless of the channel through which the cameras flow. The only negative effect could be a weakening of their dealer network. The manufacturer-approved dealers stand to lose sales to the gray market and thus would be negatively affected by Fox's entry. Fox would, of course, benefit, assuming that the entry would be a profitable operation. The consuming public would be able to buy merchandise at a lower price and would benefit, at least in the short run. Fox would be providing consumers with a mechanism to benefit from the fluctuations in the world currency market. Consumers could realize some negative effect if the gray market activities resulted in a lower quality of service for the cameras because of a weakening of the dealer network. On balance, it would appear that Fox's entry into the gray market would provide a positive net benefit in reducing the price of cameras for consumers and, thus, would be considered ethical.

The micro portion of the model, stages 2 and 3, are concerned with the action's effect on individuals. Stage 2 is concerned with the effect of the action on individuals' freedom. If the action is consistent with the rights principle, the analysis progresses to stage 3. If the individual rights are violated by the action, the action is dropped unless there is an overriding reason to continue the analysis. Only two reasons appear to be strong enough to qualify: (1) Either the NSB are of such magnitude that they outweigh the violation of individuals' rights, or (2) the potential improvement in justice is more than sufficient to offset the loss of rights.

In the case of Fox Importers, other firms could also obtain the cameras at the favorable price. The manufacturers may have agreements with their approved dealers that prohibit such action. However, that is a manufacturer-dealer problem and not Fox's. Fox should be willing to have other importers act in the same manner in which they are considering acting; that is simply smart competition. Thus, their contemplated entry into the gray market does not appear to violate the rights principle.

If stage 3 is reached, the issue of individual justice is considered. If the action satisfies the justice and rights principles, the action is accepted as ethical. If the rights principle was violated but the decision was made to continue that analysis and the justice principle was satisfied, the decision must be made as to whether the justice benefits override the rights costs. If they do, the action is accepted as ethical. If not, it is dropped. If the action fails the justice principle, it is dropped.

Fox Importers is not considering any action that would discriminate against any group. It will gain an advantage over the manufacture-approved dealers on the basis of price. However, this is a market-based decision and not unfair. Thus, based on this model, the entry into the gray market would be an ethical act. Whether it would be a smart business move would depend on the economic considerations.

Using this three-stage process, the decision maker can systematically evaluate the ethical dimension of an action with the knowledge that the resulting decisions judged to be ethical should stand up under the glare of the public spotlight. Approaching an action in this manner will not only provide ethical support for management decisions but also will upgrade the ethical awareness of business decision makers.

While normative ethical theory has been extensively developed by philosophers, there has been relatively little work done on operational ethics. For a comprehensive review of such studies in marketing, see Murphy and Laczniak (1981). We need to investigate the extent to which the ethics dimension plays a role in marketing decisions. Further, we need to learn what ethical theories are being applied to marketing decisions. We also need to develop sound, comprehensive, ethical models for the decision to use as a guide in making marketing decisions.

Managerial Issues

When operating in the international environment, ethical issues in marketing become somewhat more complex than when operating solely within the home country. While not exhaustive, the following issues should be addressed when decisions are made concerning a firm's operations in a foreign market:

Product

Is the product damaging to the people or the environment of the target market country?

Will the product enhance the lives of people in the target market country?

Promotion

Will the promotion be viewed as a bribe or a payoff by the home country or by the foreign market?

Will the promotion mislead or confuse the people in the target foreign market?

Distribution

Is a bribe or a payoff required to enter the foreign market?

What is the likelihood that an agent within the foreign market could force extortion payments for access to the market?

Price

Will the price charged in the foreign market be viewed as dumping by foreign competitors or governments?

Is the price charged in the foreign market competitively fair given current operating costs?

Conclusion

The ethical decision model, incorporating ethical principles, was presented for two reasons. First, it is hoped the model can serve as a useful guide for marketing practitioners. Second, it was presented to encourage marketing scholars to make operational normative, philosophical, and ethical principles so the principles may be used as guides in marketing decision making. The author hopes this effort will lead to more refined ethical decision models.

The extreme variations in the perceptions of the ethics of U.S. marketers emphasizes the need for U.S. marketers to upgrade their practices in the international arena. One suspects this difference in perceptions is due in part to differences in ethical behavior in the domestic and international operations of the United States. The development of ethical decision models could help upgrade the ethical practices of U.S. corporations as well as those of their foreign competitors.

References

Cavanaugh, Gerald F., Dennis J. Moberg, and Manuel Velasquez. 1981. "The Ethics of Organizational Politics." *Academy of Management Review* 6 (July), pp. 363–374.

"Common Market Sets Antidumping Duty on Some U.S. Vinyl." 1981. *The Wall Street Journal* 197 (May 19), p. 39.

"Common Market Sets 4% Antidumping Duty." 1981. *The Wall Street Journal* 197 (February 19), p. 35.

Council on Environmental Quality. 1973. *Environmental Quality: The Fourth Annual Report of the Council on Environmental Quality.* Washington, D.C.: U.S. Government Printing Office.

Fritzsche, David J., and Helmut Becker. 1984. "Linking Management Behavior to Ethical Philosophy—An Empirical Investigation." *Academy of Management Journal,* March, pp. 166–175.

"Fruitful Association: Del Monte Corp. Finds a Foreign Consultant Can Help a Great Deal." 1975. *The Wall Street Journal* 186 (July 14), pp. 1 and 19.

"Grain Concern Is Fined $500,000 in Export Case." 1976. *The Wall Street Journal* 187 (May 5), p. 8.

Murphy, Patrick E., and Gene R. Laczniak. 1981. "Marketing Ethics: A Review with Implications for Managers, Educators and Researchers." In *Review of Marketing 1981,* Ben M. Enis and K. Roering, eds. Chicago: American Marketing Association.

"Payoffs: The Growing Scandal." 1976. *Newsweek* 87 (February), pp. 26–27.

Post, James E. 1978. Testimony in *Marketing and Promotion of Infant Formula in the Developing Nations,* Hearings before the Subcommittee on Health and Scientific Research of the Committee on Human Resources, 95th Congress, Second Session, 23 May, pp. 116–125.

"Robert Buckner Had a Painful Choice to Make After Learning Sam P. Wallace Co. Paid a Bribe." 1983. *The Wall Street Journal* 108 Western Edition (May 20), p. 52.

U.S. Congress. Senate. Committee on Human Resources. Subcommittee on Health and Scientific Research. *Hearings on Marketing and Promotion of Infant Formula in Developing Nations,* 1978. Testimony of James E. Post.

Velasquez, Manual G. 1982. *Business Ethics: Concepts and Cases.* Englewood Cliffs, N.J.: Prentice-Hall, Inc.

"Watchdogs Abroad: Consumer Protection Is Underdeveloped in the Third World." 1980. *The Wall Street Journal* 195 (April 8), pp. 1 and 23.

8
Incorporating Marketing Ethics into the Organization

Gene R. Laczniak
Patrick E. Murphy

arketing decisions do have major ethical consequences. One needs only to examine the pages of metropolitan newspapers to find examples such as the following:

A major automobile manufacturer advertises rebates inflated by 25 percent because dealers are not passing their proportion of the rebates back to the customer.

A national soft drink manufacturer threatens to revoke bottler franchises if they participate in a rival competitor's legal campaign to promote a new line of soft drinks.

A major health exercise chain pretends to do telephone market research but actually conducts telephone selling.

Various organizations sell products declared unsafe (via government regulation) in the United States to other (usually less developed) countries where regulation has not determined the safety of those products.

The list of examples could go on. These few illustrations raise important issues such as misleading advertising, the use of coercive power in the channel of distribution, unethical selling and marketing research, and the sale of unsafe products.

Some marketing managers might argue that they are exempt from such ethical dilemmas or that such pressures do not affect them. In fact, a widely cited study confirms that between 65 percent and 75 percent of all managers do indeed face an ethical dilemma at some point in their career (Carroll 1975) (an ethical dilemma being defined as confronting a decision that involves sacrificing personal values for increased organizational profits). Thus, most marketing managers are not free from ethical concerns or considerations. This lends credence to the proposition that marketing decisions and their moral consequences are inextricably linked.

The Costs of Unethical Marketing

Unethical marketing decisions can have significant personal, organizational, and societal costs. Consider first the personal costs. If an action is illegal as well as unethical (as many are), the manager who makes the unethical decision can be held personally liable. Two examples illustrate this point. The Foreign Corrupt Practices Act of 1977 (which applies to U.S.-based organizations) basically prohibits the bribery of foreign officials to obtain contracts for overseas business (Kaikati and Label 1980). For each violation—that is, the payment of a bribe—the organization is subject to a $1 million fine per violation. More significant, however, the manager responsible for this payment is subject to a $10,000 fine per violation and a maximum of 5 years in prison. A second example illustrates the same point. Recent product liability cases seem to suggest that managers who knowingly decide to market unsafe products are subject to criminal and personal liability just as the organization for which they work is subject to culpability (Morgan 1982). These examples illustrate a fundamental point—namely, that unethical marketing decisions often cannot be made without the incurrence of individual responsibility by the manager involved.

There are substantial organizational costs as well. When unethical practices become known to the public, the organization will likely endure economic penalties. A sterling case in point would be the experience of the Nestlé Company with the marketing of infant formula (Sethi 1979). In that particular situation, Nestlé attempted to aggressively market infant formula as a substitute for mother's breast milk in less developed countries. Nestlé seemed to pay little attention to the fact that the proper use of infant formula required sanitary conditions and a fairly high literacy rate on the part of mothers so they could properly use the formula. Because these conditions were not present, infants incurred a substantially higher rate of malnutrition than if they had been fed mother's milk. These circumstances became known, and the result was a public relations nightmare as well as a balance sheet catastrophe for the Nestlé Company. Derogatory publicity along with a substantial loss of sales occurred due to the various boycotts of Nestlé products worldwide. (See Appendix 2D in this volume, p. 165.)

Finally, societal costs—often called *externalities*—are also generated because of unethical marketing practices. First, most unethical practices are not without their victims. For example, when consumers buy products because of misleading advertising or purchase unsafe products, they become victims of the unethical marketing practice. Many groups are particularly vulnerable to unethical selling practices, including the poor, the old, the handicapped, the mentally feeble, and recent immigrants. The disservice to these groups and others is a social cost that must be kept in mind. Second, there is damage to the workings of the economic system. Whether one believes in a free enterprise economy or a relatively planned economy, most would agree that the most

Table 8–1
Overview of Honesty and Ethical Standards
(percent)

Occupation	Very High, High	Very High	High	Average	Low	Very Low	No Opinion
Clergy	64	24	40	27	3	1	5
Druggists, pharmacists	61	14	47	33	3	1	2
Medical doctors	52	14	38	35	7	4	2
Dentists	51	8	43	41	3	2	3
College teachers	47	10	37	38	4	1	10
Engineers	45	7	38	39	2	1	13
Police officers	41	7	34	45	7	4	3
Bankers	38	5	33	49	7	2	4
TV reporters, commentators	33	5	28	47	11	4	5
Funeral directors	29	5	24	43	12	7	9
Journalists	28	4	24	47	13	4	8
Newspaper reporters	26	3	23	52	12	4	6
Lawyers	24	5	19	43	18	9	6
Stockbrokers	19	2	17	45	8	3	25
Business executives	18	3	15	55	15	5	7
Senators	16	2	14	48	21	9	6
Building contractors	18	3	15	53	18	5	6
Local political officeholders	16	2	14	49	21	8	6
Congress members	14	3	11	43	26	12	5
Realtors	13	2	11	52	21	7	7
State political officeholders	13	2	11	49	23	8	7
Insurance salespeople	13	1	12	49	22	12	4
Labor union leaders	12	2	10	35	24	20	9
Advertising practitioners	9	2	7	42	26	13	10
Car salespeople	6	1	5	34	32	23	5

Source: Gallup Poll (1983), "Honesty and Ethical Standards," *Report No. 214* (July).
Survey is based on a sample of 1,534 adults age 18 and older.

economically efficient firm rather than the most dishonest firm should be one that is rewarded. When a competitive situation with unethical marketing practices exists, the advantage in the marketplace falls to the unethical firm. Third, the confidence the public has in the profession of marketing erodes. A Gallup Poll (1983) ranked salespeople and advertising practitioners at the bottom of the ethics scale when ranking twenty-five professions (table 8–1). Because of the unethical practices of the few, all marketers are painted as hawkers, con artists, and cheats. Thus, the integrity of all marketers is called into question—a characterization that the discipline of marketing cannot afford.

The Current State of Marketing Ethics

These occurrences would not be so disturbing if it were apparent that marketers were operating at as high an ethical level as could be expected. But the evidence is somewhat to the contrary; that is, the organizational climate for marketing ethics could be clearly improved. Two relatively important studies suggest this. The findings of a survey by Ferrell and Weaver (1978) of marketing practitioners indicate that managers see their own moral values as exceeding the moral values they perceive are expected by the corporation.

A second survey, undertaken by Sturdivant and Cocanougher (1973), suggests that individuals provide a less ethical response when asked to role play a vice-president of marketing than the response they would provide when asked to play the role of a consumer. Specifically, when faced with scenarios containing ethical implications such as promoting cigarette smoking to teenagers or building a promotional campaign around a particularly obnoxious television commercial that nevertheless has high recall rates, the managers are more tolerant of the practice when they are role playing the position of the marketing executive. Together, these studies seem to present circumstantial evidence that the ethical values projected by the organization can be in conflict with the individual values held by the manager.

Recommendations for Improving Marketing Ethics in the Organization

The problem is not in finding ethical issues related to marketing or even in documenting the costs that these practices may have, but in creating organizational and decision-oriented mechanisms to deal with these problems. Too often marketing managers fall back on simplistic maxims such as the Golden Rule or vague codes of behavior. The overriding purpose of this chapter is to discuss some of the organizational and strategic mechanisms that hold the most promise for overseeing ethical performance in marketing. Special consideration is given to discussing the analysis necessary to evaluate the effectiveness of these mechanisms. The specific recommendations for improving marketing ethics are codes of marketing ethics, marketing ethics committees, and ethics education modules for marketing managers.

Codes of Marketing Conduct

A majority of large corporations have published codes of ethics. How many have specific codes of marketing ethics has never been determined, although certain sections of their general code may often apply to marketing. IBM and Quaker Oats are examples of two organizations that have sections of the corporate code that deal with specific marketing practices. At minimum, such codes reflect a nominal commitment to a proprietary operating standard by the organization. If written with care, they can provide managers with some useful operational guidelines for ethical decision making. For the organization that does not have a marketing code, the initial formulation process for such a code can improve managers' sensitivity to ethical questions.

Unfortunately, codes of ethics generally and marketing codes, in particular, often involve major problems. Codes are often viewed as primarily public relations documents, and consequently, many managers may be skeptical of their operational value to the organization. In addition, many codes are somewhat vague since they can hardly be exhaustive regarding the potential ethical problems that a manager might encounter. Furthermore, many codes are not enforced. A typical example of this is the code of ethics of the American Marketing Association (AMA), which appears on the back of the membership card. It is a six-point code, with the final point calling for the withdrawal of membership if an individual is found to be in violation of the ethical standards of the profession. Although we suspect that there have been AMA members who have engaged in unethical conduct, to the best of our knowledge no individual has ever been forced to withdraw from the AMA.

Given these problems, what can be done to assure that a code of marketing conduct has practical value to the organization? At minimum, the code of marketing conduct should have the following characteristics:

1. To avoid vagueness, the code should deal with issues that are peculiar to the industry for which the code is written. For example, toy companies must have special provisions for protecting the safety of children. Distillery firms should address the question of encouraging responsible drinking in their code of ethics. Mail order houses must address the question of their return policy and other key areas. The point is that each organization has certain areas that are particularly likely to encounter ethical abuse, and these are the areas on which the code should focus.
2. To gain the respect of managers and their subordinates, the code of marketing conduct must be enforced. Sanctions should be specified and punishments should be meted out. What the specific sanctions for a given violation would be would depend on the specific situation. For example, padding an expense account may result in a salesperson's losing his or her commission for a period of time, while a manager who induces employees to use bait-and-switch tactics constantly might be dismissed.
3. To remain current, codes should be living documents. Thus, they should be periodically revised to reflect changing environmental conditions and community standards and evolving organizational policies.

This last point strikes at one of the major advantages of marketing codes of conduct: Such documents can anticipate ethical problems and provide guidance. This contrasts with the law, which comes into play only after a violation has occurred. For example, in the case of the manager who knowingly sends out a shipment of unsafe products, that manager is guilty of an ethical violation—a breach of trust between manager and consumer. The determination of whether or not that manager is guilty of a legal violation must wait until an injury actually occurs and it is clearly shown in a court of law that the product was the direct cause of the injury.

In coming years, research dealing with ethical codes in marketing should focus on methods to make the codes more operational as well as examine the types of sanctions that seem most beneficial to making the code vital.

Marketing Ethics Committees

While many corporations have audit committees or committees on social responsibility, only a very few (for example, Norton Corporation, Monsanto, and Cummins) have a committee devoted exclusively to ethics. No corporation that we know of has a committee on marketing ethics. However, in many consumer goods companies, this might be an idea worth experimentation because it locates the responsibility for ethics with a group having expertise in the very marketing methods that might raise ethical concern. Thus, while ethics is the responsibility of everyone in the corporation, its accountability should not dissipate among the many. A specific collection of individuals should be appointed to oversee the ethical marketing climate of the organization. In order to function effectively, this marketing committee requires the following:

> The power to investigate any potential ethical abuses in marketing: These areas would range from advertising or selling practices to pricing policies and relationships with wholesalers or dealers.

> The right to ensure that any employee who offers information on organizational wrongdoing receives no career repercussions or penalties: This raises the whistle-blowing issue. As many are aware, whistle blowers have frequently been hounded from the organization of which they are a part. An example of a company that has taken a progressive position in this regard is AT&T Corporation. They have a specific policy whereby a written form is provided to new employees that tells those employees that if they ever go public with information concerning wrongdoing in the organization, they will not suffer disciplinary or retaliatory action in the future.

> The ability to adjust the code of marketing ethics: The committee would provide a logical vehicle for monitoring and updating the existing code as

well as reflecting an active commitment to ethics on the part of the firm. Organizationally, such a group could be a subcommittee of the existing internal audit team.

The duty to dole out the sanctions or punishments that might be specified by the code: Top management should give the committee the power to enforce ethical abuse.

Having an ethics committee in marketing does have disadvantages. First, it requires management time and could be perceived as a corporate police force by some members of the marketing team. Second, because some members of the marketing management team would necessarily have to be members of the committee, one would have a situation where the marketing organization was policing itself. Sometimes, such forms of self-regulation have proven to be less than effective. Nevertheless, in the future a key research issue will be to analyze the composition as well as the costs to the organization and its customers of such committees.

Ethics Education Modules for Marketing Management

The greatest commitment to high ethical standards in marketing might be reflected by holding periodic seminars for marketing managers that deal with the question of ethics. Each manager might be required to attend one such seminar every 3 or 4 years. The purpose of such educational modules would be to sensitize the marketing team to ethical problems specific to the company's operation and to imbue management with increased ethical awareness. The purpose of such seminars would not be to provide answers to ethical questions because there often are no definitive answers to ethical dilemmas. One of the few principles in the study of ethics that seems to have emerged is that levels of agreement among managers concerning what constitutes reasonable ethical conduct dissolves as the analysis moves from general to specific situations (Laczniak 1983b). Thus, the overriding purpose of the seminar would be to provide some instruction to managers on systems of moral reasoning and ethical thought.

It must be granted that the question of whether moral development in managers can be influenced is an issue that is subject to some debate. For many years the Harvard Business School subscribed to the view that a student either had ethics or did not when that student began his or her graduate studies in business. Ethics were viewed as something that could not be taught in the classroom. Similarly, one school of psychology suggests that moral development in individuals is complete by the end of the adolescent period (Munson 1979). However, contrary information exists. Some studies have suggested that courses in ethics and social responsibility have been among the most valuable to managers when the worth of graduate course work was assessed in a period of 5 to 10 years after graduation from an MBA program (Purcell 1977). Similarly, the standards of the American Assembly of Collegiate Schools of Business—the accreditation body for U.S. business schools—requires that ethics be substantially covered somewhere in the curriculum.

Concerning structure, ethics seminars would likely require an outside coordinator (consultant) who would have access to management prior to attending the seminar for the purpose of developing a company- and/or industry-specific agenda for discussion. A large part of the educational module would probably consist of case analyses of ethical issues since the case method has shown to be one of the best ways of approaching ethical discussion in business. Maximum influence would also likely occur if participants knew that an outcome of the seminar would be an appropriate modification of the company's code of ethics, by virtue of a recommendation to the standard marketing ethics committee discussed previously. Educational programs like the one described here have a heartfelt and idealistic appeal that makes them worth trying. An important future research effort will be to determine if such programs do have a measurable influence on ethical practice by marketers.

The Significance of the Marketing Vice-President

The preceding plans depend on the full and enthusiastic support of top management. One of the few undisputed findings that emerges from research concerning ethics is that the single most important factor in setting an ethical climate for the organization is the attitude of top management (Laczniak 1983a). Employees tend to look to their superiors for behavioral cues regarding how they should act in particular situations. Thus, none of the suggestions proposed can come to fruition without the enthusiastic support of top management for such changes. In smaller firms, it may be necessary that the vice-president of marketing would have to develop the code and be the ethics committee as well as the educator on ethics issues.

Conclusion

This chapter does not provide specific answers to ethical dilemmas a marketing manager might face. However, we hope these suggestions provide guidance in assisting marketing managers in becoming more sensitive to ethical considerations. That alone might be a step in the right direction. Too long marketing managers have believed that if they discharge legal responsibility, they have acted ethically. As some of the examples have illustrated, this is not always the case. Moreover, the unethical practices of marketing generate untold personal, organizational, and societal costs. These externalities should not be tolerated.

References

Baumhart, Raymond C. 1961. "How Ethical Are Businessmen?" *Harvard Business Review* (July–August), pp. 6–19 and 156–176.

Carroll, Archie B. 1975. "A Survey of Managerial Ethics: Is Business Morality Watergate Morality?" *Business and Society Review* (Spring), pp. 58–63.

Ferrell, O.C., and K. Mark Weaver. 1978. "Ethical Beliefs of Marketing Managers." *Journal of Marketing* 42 (July), pp. 69–73.

Gallup Poll. 1983. "Honesty and Ethical Standards." *Report No. 214* (July), p. 4.

Kaikati, Jack G., and Wayne A. Label. 1980. "American Bribery Legislation: An Obstacle to International Marketing." *Journal of Marketing* (Fall), pp. 38–43.

Laczniak, Gene R. 1983a. "Business Ethics: A Manager's Primer," *Business*, 33 (Jan.-Feb.-March), pp. 23–29

——— . 1983b. "Frameworks for Analyzing Marketing Ethics," *Journal of Macromarketing*, 3 (Spring), pp. 7–17.

Morgan, Fred W. 1982. "Marketing and Product Liability: A Review and Update." *Journal of Marketing* (Summer), pp. 69–78.

Munson, Howard. 1979. "Moral Thinking: Can It Be Taught?" *Psychology Today* (February), pp. 48–68, 92.

Purcell, Theodore V. 1977. "Do Courses in Business Ethics Pay Off?" *California Management Review*, 19 (Summer), pp. 50–58.

Sethi, S. Prakash. 1979. *Promises of the Good Life: Social Consequences of Marketing Decisions*. Homewood, Ill.: Richard D. Irwin, pp. 353–389.

Sturdivant, Frederick D., and A. Benton Cocanougher. 1973. "What Are Ethical Marketing Practices?" *Harvard Business Review* 51 (November–December), pp. 10–12.

Appendix 1
Codes of Ethics

This appendix presents excerpts from the codes of ethics of four corporations and two professional organizations. These codes are highlighted because one of the enduring themes of the previous chapters concerns the utility of organizations' establishing and updating formal codes of ethics. It has been argued in several instances that for those organizations not having a code, its formulation sensitizes managers to the moral implications of the decisions they make. In a related vein, for those organizations having codes, the process of code revision provides a similar benefit. The codes that were selected for inclusion in this appendix were selected to achieve several objectives. Appendix 1A, the marketing creed of the World Marketing Contact Group, represents an example of a general statement of principles. This kind of code is often a first step for many organizations in articulating their ethical responsibilities.

The codes that follow (from the Caterpillar Corporation and IBM) represent more sophisticated examples. It should be noted that the material presented in these appendixes represents abridgments of the actual codes. The excerpts that were selected were chosen to highlight the marketing dimensions of the respective corporate codes. Those interested in a full copy of the code should request one in writing from the appropriate corporate headquarters.

Two other codes are drawn from the S.C. Johnson Corporation—popularly known as the Johnson Wax Company. Appendix 1D presents Johnson's general statement of the company philosophy—one with a strong ethical orientation. Appendix 1E provides a small section from Johnson's corporate operating policy manual to show how the general sentiment of company policy is reflected in specific statements regarding product advertising.

For those particularly interested in the very sensitive area of advertising, appendix 1F presents the Code of Advertising Ethics of the American Advertising Federation.

Appendix 1G concludes this appendix with excerpts from the Code of Corporate Conduct of the ITT Corporation. Many readers may recall the ITT Company has had more than its share of criticism in the press for its hardball style of operation in the world marketplace.

Appendix 1A
World Marketing Contact Group
Marketing Creed

1. I hereby acknowledge my accountability to the organization for which I work, and to society as a whole, to improve marketing knowledge and practice, and to adhere to the highest professional standards in my work and personal relationships.

2. My concept of marketing includes as its basic principle the sovereignty of all consumers in the marketplace and the necessity for mutual benefit to both buyer and seller in all transactions.

3. I shall personally maintain the highest standards of ethical and professional conduct in all my business relationships with customers, suppliers, colleagues, competitors, governmental agencies, and the public.

4. I pledge to protect, support, and promote the principles of consumer choice, competition, and innovative enterprise, consistent with relevant legislative and public policy standards.

5. I shall not knowingly participate in actions, agreements, or marketing policies or practices which may be detrimental to customers, competitors, or established community social or economic policies or standards.

6. I shall strive to insure that products and services are distributed through such channels and by such methods as will tend to optimize the distributive process by offering maximum customer value and service at minimum cost while providing fair and equitable compensation for all parties.

7. I shall support efforts to increase productivity or reduce costs of production or marketing through standardization or other methods, provided these methods do not stifle innovation or creativity.

8. I believe prices should reflect true value in use of the product or service to the customer, including the pricing of goods and services transferred among operating organizations worldwide.

(Draft approved by WMCG in Verona, Italy, September, 1976)

9. I acknowledge that providing the best economic and social product value consistent with cost also includes: A. recognizing the customer's right to expect safe products with clear instructions for their proper use and maintenance; B. providing easily accessible channels for customer complaints; C. investigating any customer dissatisfaction objectively and taking prompt and appropriate remedial action; D. recognizing and supporting proven public policy objectives such as conserving energy and protecting the environment.

10. I pledge my efforts to assure that all marketing research, advertising, sales promotion, and sales presentations of products, services, or concepts are done clearly, truthfully, and in good taste so as not to mislead or offend customers. I further pledge to insure that all these activities are conducted in accordance with the highest standards of each profession and generally accepted principles of fair competition.

11. I pledge to cooperate fully in furthering the efforts of all institutions, media, professional associations, and other organizations to publicize this creed as widely as possible throughout the world.

Appendix 1B
Excerpts from Caterpillar Tractor Company's Code of Worldwide Business Conduct and Operating Principles

To Caterpillar People:

Large corporations are receiving more and more public scrutiny.

This is understandable. A sizable economic enterprise is a matter of justifiable public interest—sometimes concern—in the community and country where it's located. And when substantial amounts of goods, services, and capital flow across national boundaries, the public's interest is, logically, even greater.

Not surprisingly then, growth of multinational corporations has led to increasing public calls for standards, rules, and codes of conduct for such firms.

In 1974, we concluded it was timely for Caterpillar to set forth its own beliefs, based on ethical convictions and international business dating back to the turn of the century.

Experience since then has demonstrated the practical utility of this document—particularly as a means of confirming, for Caterpillar people, the company's operating principles and philosophies.

Of course, this Code isn't an attempt to prescribe actions for every business encounter. And it isn't published out of any doubt about the desire of Caterpillar people to comply with its contents. Rather, we believe that the growing size and complexity of our business—and the fact that ethical conduct isn't always subject to precise definition—argue strongly for development of such standards.

To the extent our actions match these high standards, such can be a source of pride. To the extent they don't (and we're by no means ready to claim perfection), this Code should be a challenge to each of us.

No document issued by Caterpillar is more important than this one. I trust my successors will cause it to be updated as events may merit. And I ask that you give this Code your strong support as you carry out your daily responsibilities.

Chairman of the Board
Issued October 1, 1974
Revised September 1, 1977
Revised May 1, 1982

Business Ethics

The law is a floor. Ethical business conduct should normally exist at a level well above the minimum required by law.

One of the company's most valuable assets is a reputation for integrity. If that be tarnished, customers, investors, suppliers, employees, and those who sell our products will seek affiliation with other, more attractive companies. We intend to hold to a single high standard of integrity everywhere. We will keep our word. We won't promise more than we can reasonably expect to deliver; nor will we make commitments we don't intend to keep.

The goal of corporate communication is the truth—well and persuasively told. In our advertising and other public communications, we will avoid not only untruths but also exaggeration, overstatement, and boastfulness.

Caterpillar employees shall not accept costly entertainment or gifts (excepting mementos and novelties of nominal value) from dealers, suppliers, and others with whom we do business. And we won't tolerate circumstances that produce, or reasonably appear to produce, conflict between personal interests of an employee and interests of the company.

We seek long-lasting relationships—based on integrity—with all whose activities touch upon our own.

The ethical performance of the enterprise is the sum of the ethics of the men and women who work here. Thus, we are all expected to adhere to high standards of personal integrity. For example, perjury or any other illegal act ostensibly taken to "protect" the company is wrong. A sale made because of deception is wrong. A production quota achieved through questionable means or figures is wrong. The end doesn't justify the means.

Product Quality and Uniformity

A major Caterpillar objective is to design, manufacture, and market products of superior quality. We aim at a level of quality which, in particular, offers superiority for demanding applications. We define quality as the combination of product characteristics and product support which provides optimum value to both customers and Caterpillar.

Products are engineered to exacting standards to meet users' expectations for performance, reliability, and life. Throughout the world, products are manufactured to the highest quality level commensurate with value. Our aim is to build products to identical or comparable design and quality standards, wherever they may be manufactured. Similarly, our goal is maximum interchangeability of components and parts—whatever their manufacturing source.

Product quality is constantly monitored. Our policy is to offer continuing product improvements in response to needs of customers and requirements of the marketplace.

We strive to assure users of timely after-sale parts and service availability at fair prices. From our experience, these goals are usually best achieved through locally based, financially strong, independently owned dealers committed to service. We back availability of parts from dealers with a worldwide network of corporate parts facilities. We provide a wide range of technical support to dealers to help assure high quality service for Caterpillar products.

Competitive Conduct

Fair competition is fundamental to the free enterprise system. We support laws prohibiting restraints of trade, unfair practices, or abuse of economic power. And we avoid such practices everywhere—including areas of the world where laws don't prohibit them.

In large companies like Caterpillar, particular care must be exercised to avoid practices which seek to increase sales by any means other than fair merchandising efforts based on quality, design features, productivity, price, and product support.

In relationships with competitors, dealers, suppliers, and customers, Caterpillar employees are directed to avoid arrangements restricting our ability to compete with others—or the ability of any other business organization to compete freely and fairly with us, and with others.

There must be no arrangements or understandings, with competitors, affecting prices, terms upon which products are sold, or the number and types of products manufactured or sold—or which might be construed as dividing customers or sales territories with a competitor.

In the course of our business, we may sell engines and other items to companies which are also competitors in other product areas. Related information from such customers will be treated with the same care we would expect Caterpillar data to be accorded, in a similar situation.

Relationships with dealers are established in the Caterpillar dealership agreements. These embody our commitment to fair competitive practices, and reflect customs and laws of various countries where Caterpillar products are sold. Our obligations under these agreements are to be scrupulously observed.

Caterpillar aims to increase its sales—to excel and lead. We intend to do this through superior technical skill, efficient operations, sound planning, and effective merchandising.

We believe that fair competition is good for the marketplace, customers, and Caterpillar.

Sharing of Technology

We view technology transfer in a broad context. Such transfer includes information about product and manufacturing innovations, accounting and data processing know-how, purchasing and marketing expertise—in short, all the technical and managerial knowledge needed for efficient functioning of an enterprise.

Caterpillar shares technology with employees worldwide, while observing national restrictions on transfer of such information. We also share technology with a worldwide network of suppliers and dealers. We seek the highest level of technology—regardless of origin—applicable to our manufacturing processes, products, and business generally.

Where appropriate, employees are encouraged to participate in professional and trade societies. We encourage equitable relationships with inventors, consultants, universities, and research and development laboratories having technical capabilities compatible with our needs.

One of the principal threats to future relationships among nations involves the widening gap between living standards in industrial and developing countries. Intelligent transfer of technology is a major means by which developing countries can be helped to do what they must ultimately do—help themselves.

However, technology transfer is dependent not only on the ability of people in one nation to offer it but also on the ability of people in other nations to utilize it—and their willingness to recognize that technology is valuable property. It requires time, effort, and money to create. An owner of such property is entitled to be fairly compensated for sharing it.

Countries should create an environment of law and practice that permits maximum use of transferred technology. Toward this goal, we support effective investment and industrial property laws, reasonable licensing regulations, and other measures which truly encourage transfer of technology. This goal is advanced when owners' legitimate interests are protected, and owners are permitted reasonable returns on their shared technology.

Under appropriate conditions, we enter into licensing arrangements to manufacture products locally. Such arrangements vary, depending upon products involved, scope of technical assistance required, and applicable laws and regulation. Caterpillar's products and operating methods lend themselves to licensing agreements that contemplate a continuing flow of technology. From our experience, this also produces the most benefit for host countries. Therefore, we aim at arrangements that provide continuing compensation reflecting the value of benefits generated.

Intercompany Pricing

Prices between Caterpillar companies—and between Caterpillar and affiliated companies—are established at levels equivalent to those which would prevail in "arm's length" transactions, under similar circumstances between unrelated parties. Frequently, such transactions are between Caterpillar companies in different countries. Caterpillar's intercompany pricing philosophy assures to each country a fair valuation of goods and services transferred—for tariff and income tax purposes.

Differing Business Practices

Understandably, there are differences in business practices and economic philosophies from country to country. Some of these differences are a matter of pluralism—there isn't necessarily "one best way." Other differences, however, may require changes in proven, well-accepted, fair business procedures. Such differences may be a source of continuing dispute. And they may inhibit rather than promote fair competition.

Examples of the latter include varying views regarding competitive practices, boycotts, information disclosure, international mergers, accounting procedures, tax systems, intercompany pricing, national continent requirements, product labeling, labor standards, repatriation of profit, export financing, credit insurance, and industrial property and trademark protection laws. In such areas, we favor more nearly uniform practices among countries. Where necessary, we favor multilateral action aimed at harmonizing differences of this nature.

Observance of Local Laws

A basic requirement levied against any business enterprise is that it know and obey the law. This is rightfully required by those who govern; and it is well understood by business managers.

However, a corporation operating on a global scale will inevitably encounter laws which vary widely from country to country. They may even conflict with each other.

And laws in some countries may encourage or require business practices which—based on experience elsewhere in the world—we believe to be wasteful or unfair. Under such conditions it scarcely seems sufficient for a business manager merely to say: We obey the law, whatever it may be!

We are guided by the belief that the law is not an end but a means to an end—the end presumably being order, justice, and, not infrequently, strengthening of the governmental unit involved. If it is to achieve these ends in changing times and circumstances, law itself cannot be insusceptible to change or free of criticism. The law can benefit from both.

Therefore, in a world characterized by a multiplicity of divergent laws at international, national, state, and local levels, Caterpillar's intentions fall in two parts: (1) to obey the law; and (2) to offer, where appropriate, constructive ideas for change in the law.

Reporting Code Compliance

Each officer, subsidiary head, plant or parts department manager, and department head shall prepare a memorandum by the close of each year: (1) affirming a full knowledge and understanding of this Code and (2) reporting any events or activities which might cause an impartial observer to conclude that the Code hasn't been fully followed. These reports should be sent directly to the company's General Counsel; General Offices; Peoria, Illinois.

Appendix 1C
Excerpts from IBM's
Business Conduct Guidelines

Some General Standards

The organizations we in IBM deal with include traditional customers, prospects and suppliers. But other organizations continue to emerge in our industry. They include leasing companies, software houses, distributors, dealers, banks and other financial institutions, Value Added Remarketers, equipment manufacturers, maintenance companies, third-party programmers and many others who compete with, buy from or sell to IBM.

No matter what type of organization you are dealing with, however, you should always observe these general standards:

No Misrepresentation

Don't make misrepresentations to anyone you deal with. If you believe the other person may have misunderstood you, correct any misunderstanding you find exists. Honesty is integral to ethical behavior, and trustworthiness is essential for good, lasting relationships.

Don't Use IBM's Size Unfairly

Some legitimate advantages—such as economies that derive from large-scale buying, selling and servicing—accrue to IBM because of its size. But you should never use IBM's size itself to intimidate, threaten or slight another person or organization. It has been our practice not to throw our weight around in dealing with other companies or organizations or with the public.

Reprinted with permission from *IBM Business Conduct Guidelines, Section II*, pp. 15–19. © 1983 by International Business Machines Corporation.

Treating Everyone Equitably

Everyone you do business with is entitled to fair and even-handed treatment. This is true whether you are buying, selling or performing in any other capacity for IBM.

Do not extend to another business enterprise preferential treatment such as unauthorized services or contract terms. IBM, of course, responds to competition in bidding for government and other businesses. However, if the circumstances require modified terms, they must be specifically approved by management.

IBM extends appropriate terms to each type of customer. For example, distributors, dealers and end-users all purchase certain IBM equipment under different terms. But within each category, we strive to treat equally all similarly placed customers, that is, those who are procuring in similar quantities and circumstances.

You must treat all suppliers fairly. In deciding among competing suppliers, weigh all the facts impartially, whether you are in purchasing, a branch office or some other part of the business, and whether you are buying millions of parts or a single, small repair job.

Whether or not you directly influence decisions involving business transactions, you must avoid doing anything that might create the appearance that a customer or a supplier has "a friend at IBM" who exerts special influence on its behalf.

No Reciprocal Dealing

Seeking reciprocity is contrary to IBM policy and in some cases may even be unlawful. You may not do business with a supplier of goods or of services (a bank, for example) on condition that it agrees to use IBM products or services. Do not tell a prospective customer that IBM deserves the business because of our own purchases from his or her organization.

This does not mean we cannot be supplied by an IBM customer. It does mean that IBM's decision to use a supplier must be independent of that supplier's decision to use IBM products or services.

Fairness in the Field

If you represent IBM in a marketing or service activity, the company asks you to compete not just vigorously and effectively but fairly as well. Avoid the following practices:

Disparagement

IBM relies on one thing above all to sell what it has to offer: excellence. It has long been the company's policy to provide customers the best possible products and services. Sell them on their merits, not by disparaging competitors, their products or services. False or misleading statements are improper. Avoid innuendo as well: do not "knock" the competition in an indirect way. Don't make comparisons that unfairly cast the competitor in a bad light.

In short, stress the advantages of IBM, not the disadvantages of competitors. To do otherwise only invites disrespect from customers and complaints from competitors.

Premature disclosure

IBM usually does not disclose to a particular prospect or customer anything about unannounced offerings that has not already been disclosed generally.

There are exceptions to this nondisclosure practice. One is when the national interest is involved. Another is when a customer works with IBM to develop or test new products, programs, services or distribution plans. For these and other special situations there are specific procedures for you to follow, and appropriate authorization is required in each instance.

Selling against Competitive Orders

As a matter of practice, if a competitor already has a firm order from a customer for an application, we don't market IBM products or services for that application before the competitor has installed. However, this is a complicated subject. For example, it is often difficult to determine whether a firm order actually exists. Letters of intent, free trials, conditional agreements and the like usually are not firm orders. Unconditional contracts are. Generally speaking, if a firm order does not exist, an IBM marketing representative may sell. When a situation is unclear or if there is any doubt, seek advice from your business practices or legal function.

Relations with Other Organizations

Many companies have more than one relationship with IBM. A distributor, for example, may be both a customer and a competitor of IBM. Other companies may be both competitors and suppliers. Some companies may even be suppliers, competitors, distributors and end-users of IBM products. This requires that in any dealings you have with another company, you understand the particular relationship involved.

Generally, you should deal with another organization in only one relationship at a time. If, for example, you are buying from the other company, don't try to sell at the same time. That could be a first step toward reciprocity or preferential treatment as described above. However innocently motivated, such a step should be avoided.

Business Contacts with Competitors

Be careful of your relationship with any competitor. It is inevitable that employees of IBM and its competitors will meet, talk and attend the same business meetings from time to time. Many types of contacts are perfectly acceptable when established procedures have been followed. These include sales to other companies in our industry; purchases from them; participation in approved joint bids, business shows and standards organizations and attendance at trade association functions. But even these require caution.

Prohibitions

In all contacts with competitors, the general rule is to avoid discussing such matters as pricing policy, terms and conditions, costs, inventories, product plans, market surveys or studies, production plans and, of course, any other proprietary or confidential information.

Collaboration or discussion with competitors on these subjects can be illegal. If a competitor raises any of them, even lightly or with apparent innocence, you should object, stop the discussion immediately, tell the competitor firmly that under no circumstances can you discuss these matters and, if necessary, leave the meeting.

In summary, dissociate yourself and IBM from participation in any possibly illegal activity with competitors; confine yourself to what is clearly proper and lawful. Also, report immediately to IBM legal counsel any incident associated with a prohibited subject.

Acquiring and Using Information About Others

In the normal course of doing business, you will acquire information about other companies—customers, prospects, suppliers, competitors or other organizations—including information about their employees. In itself, this is not unethical. Indeed, it can hardly be avoided. In fact, IBM quite properly gathers this kind of information for such purposes as extending credit and evaluating suppliers. The company also, quite properly, collects competitive information from a variety of publicly available sources and uses it to evaluate the relative merits of its own products, services and marketing methods. In collecting this kind of information, it is engaging in an activity that, in a competitive system, is necessary and proper.

Acquiring Information

There are limits, however, on how information should be acquired and used, especially information about competitors. No company should, through improper means, acquire a competitor's trade secrets or other confidential information.

Industrial espionage—burglary, wiretapping, stealing and so forth—is obviously wrong. So is hiring a competitor's employees to get confidential information or urging a competitor's employees or customers to disclose confidential data. IBM will not tolerate any employee's engaging in any form of questionable intelligence gathering.

Using Information

You should also be sensitive to how you use information about other companies, which often includes information about individuals. Those other companies and individuals are rightly concerned about their reputations and privacy. Adverse information of no business use should not even be retained in your files. And what information you do retain should be treated with discretion. For example, it should be communicated or made available only to those within the company who have a legitimate need to know. Also, when appropriate, in light of its nature and purpose, such information should be presented in the aggregate or in some other way to keep the identities of individuals and organizations to a minimum.

Acquiring Information from Others and Using It

Other organizations, like IBM, have intellectual property they want to protect. So do individuals. And, also like IBM, they are sometimes willing to disclose their confidential information for a particular purpose. If you are on the receiving end of another party's information, however, it is important that you proceed with caution.

Information You Believe Is Confidential

To avoid IBM's being accused of misappropriating or misusing someone's confidential information, there are certain steps you should take.

First, determine whether the information actually is confidential. This is simple enough if it is in written form and labeled confidential, or perhaps proprietary, restricted or the like, or if you are told that the information—written or oral—is confidential. If the classification is not evident but you still have some reason to believe that the information may be confidential, ask the other party.

The same precaution applies to oral information. If, before entering into a meeting or a conversation, you believe you will hear information that might be considered confidential, you should first clearly establish in writing that it is not confidential and that its use is unrestricted.

Next, you must not receive another's confidential information without the written approval of an appropriate IBM executive. Furthermore, the actual receiving of such information must not take place until the terms of its use have been formally agreed to by IBM and the other party. That means a written agreement approved by IBM legal and, usually, patent counsel. Once another party's confidential information is legitimately in your hands, you must use, copy, distribute and disclose that information only in accordance with the terms of that agreement.

Acquiring Software

One type of intellectual property that must be managed with care is software that we acquire from others, whether computer programs, data bases or related documentation. Software is often protected by a copyright or as a trade secret or confidential information. Before you accept software or sign a license agreement, you must follow established procedures.

Also, if you acquire software for your personally owned equipment, you should not copy any part of such software in any development work for IBM or, generally, bring such software onto IBM premises.

Bribes, Gifts and Entertainment

Gifts between employees of different companies range from widely distributed advertising novelties, which you may both give and receive, to bribes, which unquestionably you may not. You may pay for and accept customary business amenities such as meals, provided the expenses involved are kept at a reasonable level. Also, it frequently is necessary for a supplier, including IBM, to provide education and executive briefings for customers. It's all right to accept or provide some services in connection with this type of activity. Transportation in IBM or supplier planes to and from company locations, for instance, and lodging and food at company facilities generally are all right, although IBM normally expects its employees to use commercial carriers and facilities.

In the case of gifts, services and entertainment, however, there is a point of unacceptability. The difficulty lies in determining where that point is, unless, of course, laws make that clear.

One way to approach this question is to recognize that the purpose of both gifts and entertainment in business is to create good will. If they do more than that and *unduly influence* the recipient or make that person feel *obligated* to "pay back" the other company by giving it business, then they are unacceptable.

IBM's gift and entertainment guidelines are designed to be well within what the company believes is generally acceptable.

Receiving

Neither you, nor any member of your family, may solicit or accept from a supplier money or a gift that may reasonably be construed as having any connection with IBM's business relationship. Gifts include not just material goods but services and discounts on personal purchases of goods and services.

If you are offered money or a gift, or if one arrives at your home or office, tell your manager right away. Appropriate arrangements will be made to return or dispose of what has been received, and the supplier will be reminded of IBM's gift policy.

You may, with your manager's approval, accept a gift from a customer when the gift is of nominal value and is customarily offered to others having a similar relationship with the customer. Also, the promotional premiums and discounts offered by transportation companies, hotels, auto rental agencies and restaurants may be accepted when they are offered to travelers generally, unless IBM has specified to the contrary. Since the nature of these offerings is always changing, however, with new promotional programs being introduced frequently, IBM's practices on what may be accepted are also subject to change. You should, therefore, consult with your manager if you have any doubts regarding a specific situation.

When authorized by IBM, marketing people may refer customers to third-party vendors such as Value Added Remarketers, third-party programmers or financing houses. However, IBMers may not accept from anyone, except IBM, any fee, commission or other compensation for this activity.

Giving

You may not give money or any gift to an executive, official or employee of any supplier, customer, government agency or other organization if it could reasonably be construed as having any connection with IBM's business relationship. In countries where local customs call for giving gifts on special occasions to customers and others, you may, with appropriate prior approval, proffer gifts that are lawful, appropriate in nature and nominal in value, provided this cannot be construed as seeking special favor.

Relationships with Government Employees

What is acceptable in the business world may not be acceptable and may even be strictly against regulations in dealings with government employees. Clearly, the relevant laws governing relations between government customers and suppliers must be adhered to.

Appendix 1D
Excerpts from *This We Believe*, Johnson Wax Statement of Company Policy

The world environment in which we work and live is changing more rapidly today than ever before, leading to confusion, uncertainty and lack of confidence.

Therefore, it is important for us all to restate and reaffirm the principles which have guided us since the founding of the company.

These principles have been summarized before, in the memorable words of H.F. Johnson, Sr., during a Profit Sharing speech given on Christmas Eve, 1927:

> The goodwill of the people is the only enduring thing in any business. It is the sole substance. The rest is shadow.

The sincerity of this belief encourages us to act with integrity at all times, to respect the dignity of each person as an individual human being, to assume moral and social responsibilities early as a matter of conscience, to make an extra effort to use our skills and resources where they are most needed, and to strive for excellence in everything we do.

These principles are translated into practice through a set of basic beliefs, which relate to five groups of people to whom we are responsible, and whose trust we have to earn:

Employees: We believe that the fundamental vitality and strength of our company lies in our people.

Consumers: We believe in earning the enduring goodwill of consumers.

General Public: We believe in being a responsible leader within the free market economy.

Neighbors and Hosts: We believe in contributing to the well-being of the countries and communities where we conduct business.

World Community: We believe in improving international understanding.

Reprinted with permission.

These are our principles and beliefs. Our way of safeguarding them is to remain a privately held company. And our way of reinforcing them is to make profits through growth and development, profits which allow us to do more for all the people on whom we depend.

We believe in earning the enduring goodwill of consumers and we commit ourselves to:

Provide consumers throughout the world with useful products and services, by:

Monitoring closely the changing wants and needs of consumers.

Developing and maintaining high standards of quality.

Developing products and services which are demonstrably superior to competitive ones and which are recognizable as such by consumers.

Develop and market products which are environmentally sound, and which do not endanger the health and safety of consumers, by:

Meeting all regulatory requirements or exceeding them where company standards are higher.

Providing clear and adequate directions for safe use, together with cautionary statements and/or symbols.

Incorporating protection against misuse where this is appropriate.

Researching new technologies for products which favor an improved environment.

Maintain and develop comprehensive consumer education and service programs, by:

Disseminating consumer information which promotes full understanding of company products and their correct use.

Handling all consumer inquiries, complaints and service needs quickly, thoroughly and fairly.

We believe in being a responsible leader within the free market economy, and we commit ourselves to:

Conduct our business in a fair and ethical manner, by:

Not engaging in unfair business practices.

Treating our suppliers and customers both fairly and reasonably, according to sound commercial practice.

Packaging and labeling our products so that consumers can make an informed value judgment.

Maintaining the highest advertising standards of integrity and good taste.

Not engaging in bribery.

Appendix 1E
Excerpts from the Johnson Wax Corporate Policy Manual: Product Advertising and Advertising Policy

Background/Objectives

We participate in competitive businesses in which the consumer or user has a choice of many products besides our own. It is the role of advertising to inform the public about our products and their benefits so that the consumer can make an intelligent, informed buying decision.

While our Company image and reputation with the general public is based primarily on product performance, we recognize that it is also influenced by the quality and effectiveness of our product advertising.

Policy

1. Product advertising will inform the potential users about our products and their benefits so they can make an intelligent, informed buying decision.

2. Advertising will be truthful. It will not over-promise or create unrealistic expectations about the performance of our products. Performance and other claims, either actual or implied, will be substantiated by appropriate technical or consumer support.

3. All product advertising will be in good taste. It should not be inconsistent with our image, or cause consumers to react unfavorably, or portray people in a demeaning or embarrassing manner, or make unfair, misleading, inaccurate or disparaging statements about competitors or their products.

4. Product advertising is a reflection of our Company, and it should not be placed in media which will offend generally accepted standards of propriety and decency or which present highly controversial subject matter in a biased or exploitive way. "Media," in this context, could be, for example,

either a magazine or a particular issue of that magazine; a television program or a particular episode of that program.

5. Each company will be aware of, and responsive to, national concerns, for example, the representation of appropriate ethnic or other minorities in their product advertising.

Definition

Product advertising is whatever the company says or shows about our products to the public, especially through such media as television, newspapers, magazines, radio, billboards, brochures and the like, whether consumer or trade oriented. It also includes product advertising communicated through labels, packages, and sales promotion materials.

Practices

Each company will establish its own procedures for the approval of all forms of product advertising before such advertising is released. The approval will include review by R&D, legal and other functions, as appropriate.

The responsibility for maintaining the product advertising standards described in this policy is with the general manager of a subsidiary company, and the appropriate Operations head for U.S. Consumer Products and for U.S. Innochem operations.

Advertising Policy

During the early days of radio and TV, the Company sponsored its own programs. This practice assured us that the program environment was not incompatible with our commercials. Today, like most other advertisers, the Company no longer sponsors its own programs; our commercials appear on many different programs. The following policy guides our selection of these programs from among those offered by the networks and other suppliers of TV entertainment.

Policy

As a responsible television advertiser, Johnson Wax will actively seek out programs which not only satisfy our specific advertising needs, but also support and enhance our reputation as a socially responsible corporation. We recognize that most programs made available to us will not satisfy both of these objectives, since much of what is on television must appeal to a wide range of interests, tastes and preferences. However, in selecting from available programs, we will specifically avoid those whose appeal is based on excessive violence or the manifest exploitation of controversial subjects; additionally, we will take care to insure that the content of programs on which we advertise is appropriate to the time period in which they are shown.

Implementing Guidelines

In carrying out this policy, we and advertising agencies acting in our behalf will avoid placing our advertising on programs or program episodes which could be characterized as follows:

Programs which include violence for its own sake and when it makes no significant contribution to the understanding of the story line.

Programs which sensationalize acts of brutality or human suffering through overly realistic presentation.

Programs which dramatize anti-social actions in a manner that might encourage or stimulate imitations.

Programs which involve the discussion of subjects or depiction of behavior which is of a highly controversial nature in an exploitive manner, including exploitive depiction of human sexuality.

We believe this course is in our self-interest as a company making quality consumer products and also in the interest of the public at large.

Practices

Selection of programs on which the company will place its advertising will be made by the Director of Advertising Services, who will adhere to the above implementing guidelines. In instances where a proposed program "buy" may appear to conflict with one or more of the guidelines, the Director of Advertising Services and the Director of Public Affairs will preview the program to determine whether it fits within this policy.

Appendix 1F
American Advertising Federation's
Code of Advertising Ethics

1. Truth—advertising shall reveal the truth, and shall reveal significant facts, the omission of which would mislead the public.
2. Substantiation—advertising claims shall be substantiated by evidence in possession of the advertiser and the advertising agency prior to making such claims.
3. Comparisons—advertising shall refrain from making false, misleading, or unsubstantiated statements or claims about a competitor or his products or services.
4. Bait Advertising—advertising shall not offer products or services for sale unless such offer constitutes a bona fide effort to sell the advertised products or services and is not a device to switch consumers to other goods or services, usually higher priced.
5. Guarantees and Warranties—advertising of guarantees and warranties shall be explicit, with sufficient information to apprise consumers of their principal terms and limitations or, when space or time restrictions preclude such disclosures, the advertisement shall clearly reveal where the full text of the guarantee or warranty can be examined before purchase.
6. Price Claims—advertising shall avoid price claims which are false or misleading, or savings claims which do not offer provable savings.
7. Testimonials—advertising containing testimonials shall be limited to those of competent witnesses who are reflecting a real and honest opinion or experience.
8. Taste and Decency—advertising shall be free of statements, illustrations, or implications which are offensive to good taste or public decency.

Reprinted with permission.

Appendix 1G
Excerpts from the ITT Code
of Corporate Conduct

Responsibility for Adherence to ITT Code of Corporate Conduct and Other Policies and Standard Practices of ITT

To All ITT Managers:

The above Code states that it is your job, your responsibility, to adhere to ITT's Code of Corporate Conduct and to ensure that those you supervise know and adhere to the policies contained therein. It is important to understand this. The primary responsibility for compliance rests with line management—not with the lawyers, or the controllers, or the auditors, though each is available to assist the manager—and this responsibility cannot be delegated!

ITT Business Practices

As an ITT manager, you are responsible for ensuring that all ITT employees under your supervision perform their duties in accordance with the highest standards of business ethics and in conformance with applicable law.

You are to take every action necessary to ensure that no ITT entity or employee engages directly or indirectly in any corrupt business practice, including bribery, kickbacks, or payoffs.

With reference to the use of sales agents, you will use only those who operate legitimate independent businesses.

Use of ITT funds and assets under your control is your responsibility. These funds and assets are not to be used for other than legitimate, ethical business purposes. You will assure that no false or artificial corporate records are made and that there are no unrecorded corporate assets.

As you know, ITT System employees having knowledge of facts indicating violation of this Policy are required to report the matter to the Director—Corporate Policy Compliance—ITT.

Conflict of Interest

As long as you remain an ITT employee, your duty is to act in business matters solely for the benefit of the Corporation. Your salary and other corporate benefits are full compensation for your services to ITT. You must particularly avoid any act on behalf of ITT which might produce an unauthorized private financial benefit for yourself, your family, friends or business associates.

You and those under your supervision must not become involved for personal gain with competitors, customers or suppliers to the ITT System.

Use of Representatives by ITT System Units

As an ITT manager you must ensure that every agreement with sales agents or representatives is in writing, signed by the parties, contains all terms agreed upon, and conforms to the requirements above. The agent, its employees, and owners must be engaged in providing legitimate business services for a fee not in excess of the customary local rate for services, and be free of involvement with existing or potential customers of ITT. Any payment made to sales agents or representatives must be fully documented.

You will use reasonable vigilance to assure that no ITT System employee, and no agent, directly or indirectly, makes or authorizes any payment or gift to any representative of a potential or actual government or commercial customer for the purpose of obtaining or retaining business for, or directing business to, any entity.

Safety of ITT Products

We at ITT have a duty to provide products to our customers which are safe for intended use and foreseeable misuse, and which comply with all applicable laws, regulations and standards. You must ensure the accomplishment of this objective by implementing a formal Product Safety Program customized to your specific needs.

Appendix 2
Cases

This appendix presents four case studies for those who wish to apply some of the guidelines that were discussed in previous chapters to real world case situations. It should be stated at the outset that these case histories were not chosen as clear-cut examples of unethical behavior. In fact, quite the contrary, each of these cases, with one possible exception, raises a legitimate issue of whether an ethical trust has been violated at all.

The first case, Heublein, Inc., deals with a line of milk-flavored, alcoholic products that Heublein offered to the public in the late 1970s. An ethical issue soon arose: Would a line of alcoholic drinks with flavors such as strawberry, mocha, banana, and chocolate mint provide a temptation for children to experiment with alcoholic beverages?

The second case, General Motors, deals with the infamous engine-switching incident. In this instance, General Motors replaced numerous Oldsmobile engines in Oldsmobile automobiles with Chevrolet power plants. When consumers who purchased cars found out about this engine switch, they were upset. General Motors maintained that the difference between the Chevrolet engine and the Oldsmobile engine was negligible. Consumers retorted that they had been promised a unique Oldsmobile engine and that the substitution of a Chevrolet engine without their permission, in fact, constituted a case of consumer fraud. This and some related issues surrounding these incidents provide considerable substance for ethical debate.

The third case deals with the Giant Foods supermarket chain and some of the merchandising changes it made when the organization instituted the wide-scale use of optical scanners. Significantly, Giant Foods has always had the reputation of being one of the most consumer-oriented retailers in the United States. With the advent of these scanners and the inclusion of Universal Product Codes (UPCs) on most products, Giant Foods, for purposes of efficiency, moved away from marking a specific sticker price on individual food items. The question became, did the removal of such price information, although it was posted on the shelf as well as the final check-out tape, violate the consumer's right to information?

The fourth case deals with the celebrated marketing campaign for infant formula in Third World countries. While the general marketing campaign conducted by Nestlé Corp. was widely condemned in its aftermath as being unethical, it is interesting to note that no specific laws were violated in the orchestration of the campaign. This raises the significant question of whether a firm that acts within the technicalities of the law has, in fact, discharged its ethical and social responsibility.

Appendix 2A
Heublein, Inc., A
Socially Questionable Product

S tuart D. Watson, chairman of the board at Heublein, Inc., sat in his office to review a speech he was to give that evening. The occasion was the annual meeting of the Wine Institute, a trade association of wine producers and distributors. Watson had selected as his topic, "The Corporate Responsibilities at Heublein." He would focus in the speech on the importance of monitoring the social and political environment for contingency planning purposes.

In particular, Watson intended to discuss the role at Heublein, Inc., of public affairs and the Corporate Responsibility Committee. Watson was proud of the research sponsored by Heublein on the causes and treatment of alcoholism. He was also pleased that the Corporate Responsibility Committee had provided strong guidance to senior executives on advertising, product, and distribution policies. As an example of the Committee's efforts, he intended to show some recent advertisements that were sensitive to the social consequences of alcohol consumption. The ads depicted people with and without cocktails, all having fun. The intention was not to glamorize drinking as the socially desirable thing to do. The text of the ads stressed moderation.

Just as Watson completed his review, he received a call from John J. Moran, vice president of public affairs. Moran began by saying, "Stuart, did you see the Today Show this morning? Well, I did. I could not believe my eyes. Betty Furness got some fifth graders drunk on Cows and then told America, 'This proves that Heublein is trying to appeal to kids.' Stuart, we cannot let this one lie like we did in November with the MacNeil-Lehrer Report." Watson agreed and asked Moran to prepare his recommendations for an appropriate response. He further requested Moran to add the issue to the agenda of the Corporate Responsibility Committee meeting scheduled for the following day.

From Roy Adler/Larry Robinson/Jan Carlson, *Marketing and Society: Cases and Commentaries,* © 1981, pp. 30, 32, 34–39. Reprinted by permission of Prentice-Hall, Inc., Englewood Cliffs, N.J.

Company Background

Heublein, Inc., was, in 1977, the largest producer and distributor of distilled spirits and wines in the United States. Corporate-wide revenue was over $799 million for the first half of fiscal 1977. Table 2A-1 shows a steady growth pattern in both revenues and profits for the period 1972–1976. Prior to 1976, the company was organized in three major profit centers: beverage, food, and international. In January 1976, the company reorganized into five groups: spirits, wines, food service and franchising, grocery products, and international. Of these, spirits was the largest, in both sales and profits, with 1976 sales over $300 million and profits of approximately $35 million.

The Heublein product line featured over 200 well-known consumer product brand names, including Smirnoff Vodka, Black and White Scotch, A-1 Steak Sauce, Ortega Chiles and Sauces, Italian Swiss Colony, Lancers, Inglenook, Annie Green Springs, T.J. Swann, Jose Cuervo Tequilla, Black Velvet Canadian Whiskey, Irish Mist, Harvey's Bristol Cream, and Snap-E-Tom Cocktails. In addition, the company had acquired, in 1971, Kentucky Fried Chicken.

Heublein had been plagued by several serious problems in recent years which had the net effect of plummeting Heublein stock from 40½ down to the 20s, even though sales and profits continued to be strong. The Christmas quarter of 1976, normally the strongest sales period, was disappointing, with sales down by 13 percent from the previous year. Preliminary estimates showed that company profits for the first half of the fiscal year 1977 would be up only 1 percent over the previous year.

Several reasons were cited by management for the declining performance of company products. First, in 1975, the Federal Trade Commission challenged Heublein's acquisition of United Vintners, a prestigious and profitable wine group, second only to the E&J Gallo Winery in market share. In negotiations with the FTC, Heublein offered to divest itself of the Petri, Italian Swiss Colony, and Lejon product lines while retaining the Inglenook, T.J. Swann, and Annie Green Springs brands. The FTC rejected this proposal and the case was expected to go to court in late 1977.

Another problem area had been the declining performance of Kentucky Fried Chicken (KFC). As of June 1976, the KFC chain included 4,340 company-owned or franchised outlets, which spent over $30 million on advertising. KFC ranked second in fast-food-industry sales, behind McDonald's, and the company had planned to retain this position by relying on its superior marketing capabilities in spite of a trend of continuous and substantial price increases. Problems occurred when, as one industry analyst put it, "the oil shortage and the nation's economic problem resulted, the economics of a burger meal for the family began to look a lot more attractive than a $9 bucket of chicken . . . they priced themselves into a bind."[1] KFC planned to

Table 2A–1
Heublein, Inc. Consolidated Summary of Operations
(dollars in thousands)

	1976	1975	1974	1973	1972
Revenues					
Beverage	$858,706	$772,576	$697,018	$586,423	$507,125
Food	489,302	446,792	387,272	315,096	273,154
International	235,125	195,047	155,852	64,620	33,721
	1,583,133	1,414,415	1,240,142	966,139	814,000
Cost of sales	1,099,416	988,474	855,134	660,173	546,674
Selling, advertising, administrative, and general expenses	338,454	290,151	265,660	211,523	181,185
Operating income	$145,263	$135,790	$119,348	$94,443	$86,141
Operating income					
Beverage	$72,732	$63,226	$52,044	$42,005	$39,080
Food	52,211	55,985	51,458	45,170	43,456
International	20,320	16,579	15,846	7,268	3,605
	145,263	135,790	119,348	94,443	86,141
Interest expense	18,494	16,910	9,830	6,357	7,381
Interest income	2,810	2,147	1,384	1,683	646
Miscellaneous income (expense)—net	763	632	122	(225)	367
Income taxes	64,433	61,661	58,683	46,877	41,474
Income from continuing operations	65,909	59,998	52,341	42,667	38,299
Income (loss) from discontinued operations, less tax effect	7,184	1,498	2,069	1,544	(607)
Income before extraordinary items	73,093	61,496	54,410	44,211	37,692
Extraordinary items, less tax effect	—	—	—	(13,800)	(15,250)
Net income	73,093	61,496	54,410	30,411	22,442
Preferred dividends	—	—	—	—	293
Earnings applicable to common stock	73,093	61,496	54,410	30,411	22,149
Common and common equivalent shares	$21,536,526	$21,216,540	$21,166,002	$20,932,055	$19,607,538
Earnings per common and common equivalent share					
Continuing operations	$3.06	$2.83	$2.47	$2.04	$1.94
Discontinued operations	0.33	0.07	0.10	0.07	(0.03)
Before extraordinary items	3.39	2.90	2.57	2.11	1.91
Extraordinary items	—	—	—	(0.66)	(0.78)
Net earnings	$3.39	$2.90	$2.57	$1.45	$1.13

Source: Heublein Annual Report (May, 1978), pp. 17–18.

reduce prices and return to emphasizing a smaller sales package to recapture its declining market share.

The spirits groups also suffered problems during this period. The Black Velvet Whiskey campaign was given the "Keep Her in Her Place" Advertising Award in 1974 by the National Organization for Women for a campaign described as a demeaning "sex-sell." This was followed by an attack from the Oregon State Liquor Commission for "sexually suggestive" advertising.[2] Black and White Scotch, the leading brand of scotch in the 1950s, acquire by Heublein in 1974, experienced a decreasing market share. The company found itself unable to stop the decline. The trend, averaging a decrease of 110,000 cases per year since 1974, represented a drain on corporate profitability.

On the positive side, Heublein had Smirnoff Vodka, which was acquired in 1939 for a mere $14,000 and a small royalty by John G. Martin, grandson of Heublein's founder. Smirnoff was the largest selling vodka in the country, with sales of 5.5 million cases in 1976. Smirnoff accounted for nearly $15 million in profits in 1976. Smirnoff was the most heavily advertised distilled spirits product in the industry, as suggested by table 2A–2.

Beyond its more traditional liquor lines, Heublein was the industry leader in the prepared cocktail market, with a market share of over 75 percent. Although experts tended to see the company's expertise primarily in marketing, Heublein's research and development division was the largest and most active in the liquor industry. Researchers worked on developing and testing new products ranging from bottled martinis, manhattans, and canned whiskey sours through plum and peach wines to the "softer" coffee and chocolate liqueurs.

Over 1,000 ideas were generated by the marketing department and other sources throughout the year, and of that number, perhaps 100 were considered practical from a marketing or production viewpoint. The time span from conception to full distribution often took several years. A new product had to be salable and also retain quality and flavor over the months it might sit on a store shelf. Thirteen new drinks were introduced in 1974, the success of which contributed to the spirits division market increase from 9.9 percent to over 13 percent of the total market for distilled spirits.

Table 2A–2
Advertising Expenditures for Distilled Spirits,
1976 Leading 10 Brands, Magazines

Product	Expenditures
1. Smirnoff	$4,067,353
2. Johnnie Walker	3,678,147
3. Canadian Club	3,614,095
4. J & B	3,423,641
5. Chivas Regal	2,817,170
6. Seagram's V.O.	2,390,809
7. Dewar's	2,298,070
8. Hereford's Cows	2,195,269
9. Beefeater	2,146,536
10. Heublein Cocktails	2,102,771

Source: *1977 Liquor Handbook* (New York: Gavin-Jobson Associates, 1977):320.

Table 2A-3
Distilled Spirits Products, Percentage Sales Increases, 1961–1980

Product	1961–1966	1966–1971	1971–1976	1976–1980	1961–1976
Wine	25.4	29.9	11.5	—	+ 81.68
Vodka	58.6	51.6	55.4	55.4	+ 273.6
Gin	37.7	18.9	4.4	4.4	+ 70.9
Canadian whiskey	66.9	70.6	31.4	31.4	+ 274.0
Scotch	55.1	54.5	8.2	8.2	+ 159.1
Brandy/cognac	46.5	41.3	15.2	15.2	+ 138.5
Prepared cocktails	109.7	30.3	113.5	113.5	+ 483.7
Rum	57.8	77.1	43.1	43.1	+ 300.1

Source: *1977 Liquor Handbook* (New York: Gavin-Jobson Associates, 1977):280–319.

Heublein noted a sharp trend toward lighter and sweeter drinks, with lower alcohol content. As shown in table 2A–3, the prepared cocktail market was growing at over 20 percent per year. The forecast for 1976–1980 showed a continued trend for this category of distilled spirits. As a result, Heublein had its R&D division working on new prepared cocktail drinks. One result was the introduction in 1975 of Malcolm Hereford's Cows—a sweet 30-proof, milk-type drink—first conceived 6 years earlier.

Hereford's Cows was test marketed in Chicago in the spring of 1975.[3] The product was available in five flavors—banana, strawberry, coconut, chocolate mint, and mocha. The successful results of the Chicago test market led to a decision to distribute nationally in March 1976. The product had originally been targeted for women in the age group 18 to 35. It was subsequently found to have strong appeal for other groups as well, including blacks, young males, and women over 35. Hereford's Cows was budgeted for over $3 million in advertising for 1976.

The product achieved market acceptance far in excess of forecasted levels. In fact, with first-year sales at over a million cases, it was the most successful distilled spirits new product introduction in the history of the industry. William V. Elliott, vice president, marketing, stated:

> There's a huge market here because Cows even appeal to non-drinkers. . . .
> We could spend triple our promotional budget and it still won't be enough
> . . . . The repeat business on this product has been phenomenal.[4]

Having seen the success of Cows' appearance on the market, Heublein introduced Kickers, a product almost identical to Cows except for packaging. Kickers was designed to increase demand for milk-type "fun" drinks by appealing to those individuals who considered themselves energetic, activity-minded, and "young at heart."

The Controversy

Robert MacNeil, in the introduction to a November 5, 1976, airing of the MacNeil-Lehrer Report on the subject of teenage alcoholism, said:

> The appearance of Cows and similar drinks from other manufacturers has alarmed doctors and others concerned with alcoholism. In particular, they are worried that these pop drinks will exacerbate an already serious social problem, teenage drinking.[5]

The show, which focused on Heublein's 30-proof Hereford's Cows, represented a summation of the social objections which surfaced shortly after the product was successfully test marketed and introduced nationally.

Susan Papas, a spokesperson for Odyssey House, a New York center for the rehabilitation of teenage alcoholics, said the sweet-tasting Cows "can cause the start or beginning of teenage problems." She explained:

> Kids that don't like Scotch or Vodka or other types of hard liquors might be more inclined to drink something that is like a milkshake. And milk is a very acceptable form of something to drink. And with a bottle like this, that's equal to two and a half cans of beer, I think they probably get a little surprised very quickly.[6]

Although Papas admitted that she had no statistics on Cows specifically, she said her experiences at Odyssey House taught her that teenage alcoholics begin by drinking sweet-tasting products. "It's the pop, the lightness; it's the way it's presented."[7]

In addition to objecting to the ready accessibility of these drinks to potential young alcoholics, Papas and others cited advertising that promoted alcohol as the answer to numerous adult situations, "which happen to be the very ones that teenagers find particularly frightening and painful."[8]

Referring to one of Heublein's ads for Kickers, a companion product to the Cows, Nicholas Pace, assistant professor of medicine at New York University-Bellevue Medical Center, president of the New York City Affiliate of the National Council on Alcoholism, and chairman of the New York State Advisory Commission on Alcoholism, told Robert MacNeil:

> It seems as if an awful lot of Madison Avenue . . . is sort of geared towards showing the use of the drug alcohol in a romantic way that would allow people an escape or a method to dull their senses or to increase their sexual activity and so on.[9]

Other individuals active in fighting alcoholism objected to Heublein's attitude. Morris Chafetz, a medical psychiatrist who was a former head of the National Institute on Alcohol Abuse and Alcoholism, stated:

I must say that I am concerned about the Cow drinks. Not because I think they are designed to hook people to alcoholic problems, but because it reflects a lack of sensitivity on the part of the liquor industry.[10]

He further stated:

The liquor industry could be moving ahead faster . . . It's taking them a little longer to learn that there is no advantage to their product in people suffering from alcohol abuse and alcoholism.[11]

Pace, Chafetz, and Papas all agreed that they didn't believe government regulation of business practices and advertising was the answer to the types of problems they saw represented in Heublein's Cow. Chafetz, in summary, stated that he believed that the people in the liquor industry "are socially responsible and I would like them to downplay their product or remove it."[12]

Heublein did not respond publicly to the allegations and comments made on the MacNeil-Lehrer Report.

Heublein, the manufacturer of Hereford's Cows, declined to send a representative to join us tonight. A company spokesman objected that this program "was making a direct reference to certain products and had already made a decision that we (that's Heublein) were part and parcel of the problem." The Heublein man added, "It's like we're being placed on trial. Besides we had late notice." In fact, our reporter first contacted Heublein a week ago. We should note that Heublein also refused to send a representative to a Senate hearing on this subject last March. The industry's main lobbying organization in Washington, the Distilled Spirits Council of the United States, also declined to join us. So did the advertising agency that handles the Cows account, and the American Association of Advertising Agencies. The U.S. Brewers Association and the Association of National Advertisers did not respond to our phone calls.[13]

In response to objections raised that advertisements for Kickers seemed to be primarily directed at teenagers, Heublein dropped its advertising campaign even though it disputed the complaint. A spokesman for the Institute of Alcohol Abuse later stated that "Heublein acted very responsibly in acknowledging our concern about the problem of teen drinking, which appears on the rise."[14]

The current crisis occurred against this background. Betty Furness, former Special Assistant for Consumer Affairs to President Johnson and currently consumer affairs reporter for NBC-TV, handed out Dixie cups filled with a beverage which later was found to be Strawberry Hereford's Cows to a classroom of 12- to 14-year-olds.[15] The students were unaware that the cups contained an alcoholic beverage. This action was taped for a segment on

NBC's Today show to back up earlier statements made by Furness in criticism of Heublein products.

In an effort to prove that kids were attracted by advertising for sweet milk-type drinks, and without disclosing her intentions to either school officials or the students' parents, Furness gave the teenagers a cup of the beverage. She then recorded their enthusiastic responses to her question of whether they preferred the sweet-cream Cows "rather than a shot of scotch." Furness closed the Today show segment with the statement: "This is proof that Heublein is trying to appeal to young people." Furness did not question the students about whether they had seen any of the advertisements being challenged or if they had heard of the product.

The Alternatives

Moran hung up the phone after his brief conversation with Watson. He began to consider the options available to Heublein in response to the latest incident involving the Hereford Cows.

Before laying out the alternatives, Moran reviewed the data provided by research and development and by marketing on the Hereford Cows. First, it was clear that most people could not drink more than two or three Cows at one sitting. The product was quite sweet and had a milk base. In fact, research in the R&D laboratory showed a high probability that a drinker would get physically sick before he or she would become drunk. Also, marketing research showed that the primary adopters of the product were 25-to 39-year-old women.[16] Further, an awareness study showed that only 8 percent of teenagers polled were aware of the product. Perhaps of most importance, the retail price of Cows, $4.50 to $6.00 per fifth, was well above the cost of the alcohol products typically consumed by teenage alcoholics. These data suggested to Moran that the charges were without factual basis.

He looked at his watch. It was nearly noon. The Corporate Responsibility Committee meeting was scheduled for 8:00 A.M. the following day. That left little time to prepare his recommendations for response to the latest incident which threatened the continued success of the Malcolm Hereford's Cows line of packaged cocktails.

Notes

1. "Top 100 Advertisers," *Advertising Age,* August 18, 1976, pp. 145–146.
2. Ibid.
3. The details that follow were drawn from John J. O'Connor, "Heublein's Hereford's Cows Success Tips Marketers to Hot New Liquor Area," *Advertising Age,* December 1, 1976, pp. 1, 75.

4. Ibid.

5. "Teenage Alcoholism," *The MacNeil-Lehrer Report,* Library No. 290, Show No. 245, November 4, 1976.

6. Ibid.

7. Ibid.

8. Ibid.

9. Ibid.

10. Ibid.

11. Ibid.

12. Ibid.

13. Ibid.

14. The account of the incident was drawn from Mitchell C. Lynch, "The Day All the Kids Got Booze in Class from Betty Furness," *The Wall Street Journal,* February 12, 1978, pp. 1, 30.

15. Ibid.

16. "The Furness Fiasco," *Advertising Age,* February 6, 1978, p. 16.

Appendix 2B
General Motors:
The Engine Switch Controversy

Douglas J. Dalrymple

In early March 1977, Joe Siwek took his new Delta 88 Oldsmobile to his Chicago dealer to have the fan belt replaced. There was some delay in repairing the car because it was found to be equipped with a Chevrolet engine. The Chevy engine required a slightly different fan belt than the similar Oldsmobile Rocket engine and the dealer did not have one in stock.

The standard engine for the 1977 Oldsmobile Delta 88 was a 231 cubic inch V-6 manufactured by the Buick Division of General Motors. Oldsmobile also offered an optional 350 cubic inch V-8 engine for the Delta 88 for an additional charge of $190. In past years, Delta 88's were equipped with Rocket engines manufactured by the Oldsmobile Division. It was clear before the introduction of the 1977 cars, however, there would not be enough 350 Rocket engines to power all the redesigned Delta 88 models. The shortage was caused by the use of the 350 Rocket engine block to make a 403 cubic inch V-8 for use in larger Buicks, Oldsmobiles, and Pontiacs. Due to the strong demand for these cars (table 2B–1), there were not enough 350 Rocket engine blocks to go around. General Motors resolved the problem by installing 350 cubic inch Chevrolet V-8 engines in about half of the Oldsmobile Delta 88 cars.

Before the 1977 models were introduced, Oldsmobile notified its dealers that a different engine would be used in Delta 88 cars sold in parts of the United States. Advertising for 1977 Delta 88 cars mentioned the availability of a 350 V-8 with a 4 barrel carburetor, but did not refer to the Olds Rocket engine. Some promotional material prepared prior to the introduction of the Delta 88s contained references to the Rocket engine and the material was reprinted to delete the Rocket reference.

This case was prepared by Associate Professor Douglas J. Dalrymple of Indiana University as a basis for class discussion rather than to illustrate either effective or ineffective handling of an administrative situation. From Douglas J. Dalrymple and Leonard J. Parsons, *Marketing Management: Text and Cases*, 2nd ed., copyright © 1980 by John Wiley and Sons. Reprinted by permission of John Wiley and Sons, Inc.

Table 2B-1
Automobile Sales, by Selected Manufacturers
(1,000)

Manufacturer	1974	1975	1976
General Motors Corporation			
Oldsmobile Division	525	636	901
Buick Division	430	518	738
Pontiac Division	497	503	753
Cadillac Division	224	267	304
Chevrolet Division	2,019	1,822	2,104
Ford Motor Company			
Ford Division	1,787	1,542	1,715
Total Sales			
U.S. Manufacturers	7,449	7,050	8,607

Source: *Wall Street Journal,* January 7, 1975, p. 5; January 8, 1977, p. 3.

Because Siwek thought his car was equipped with the Olds Rocket engine, the Chicago dealer offered to trade him another 1977 Delta 88 with an Olds 350 engine. The replacement car had been owned by the dealer and had fewer miles on it than Siwek's car. Before the paperwork on the exchange could be completed, however, Siwek complained to the Chicago Consumer Advocate's Office. As the result of this complaint, the Illinois Attorney General filed a class action lawsuit against General Motors, charging it deceived consumers by not informing them of the engine switch. After the suit was announced, 250 additional complaints were received from Illinois car buyers describing engine substitutions with Oldsmobiles, Pontiacs, Buicks, and Cadillac Sevilles. Portions of the Illinois Consumer Fraud Act and the Uniform Deceptive Trade Practices Act have been reproduced in Appendix A.

The publicity surrounding the Illinois lawsuit awakened the consumer activists around the country, and soon over 256 lawsuits had been filed against General Motors by states and individuals. General Motors denied they deceived consumers and pointed out that both the Olds and Chevy engines were virtually identical in size and performance and carried the same GM warranty. Also, because the 350 engines were optional equipment, their installation helped fill a customer request.

General Motors strongly defended engine sharing among its divisions both in terms of production economics and savings on tests for pollution controls. Engine sharing is expected to increase in the future because of the high costs of certifying a variety of engines to meet government pollution and gas mileage standards. The widespread nature of engine sharing is shown by the use of the standard Delta 88 engine, a 231 V-6 manufactured by Buick, in 13 separate car lines sold by Buick, Oldsmobile, and Pontiac. Chevrolet is the only division of General Motors that makes all of its own engines. In addition, General Motors has followed a policy of sharing car bodies among its Chevrolet, Buick, Oldsmobile, and Pontiac Divisions for many years. Although the outside sheet metal is different across divisions, the frame and body components are virtually identical. This sharing of body components is a holdover from the time when all GM car bodies were manufactured by the Fisher Body Division of the Company. At the Ford Motor Company, the same engines are used by the Ford and Lincoln-Mercury Division, and Dodge, Chrysler, and Plymouth cars also share engines.

Because of the confusion over the 350 engines, General Motors ran newspaper ads in late March of 1977 in the 50 largest markets explaining its engine lineup and indicating that its 350 engines were made by Chevrolet, Buick, Oldsmobile, Pontiac, and GM of Canada. GM also advised its Olds dealers to carry parts for routine service and maintenance of the Chevy engines and began labeling the cars to identify those with the Chevy 350 engines. General Motors assured the attorney general in Michigan that buyers of the 350 powered cars would be contacted by letter and provided with detailed specifications on the engine installed in each car.

One issue presented by consumer groups to support their case against General Motors was the difference in the EPA mileage figures reported for the two engines. Federal figures show the Delta 88 equipped with the Chevy engine was rated at 15 miles-per-gallon in the city and 20 mpg on the highway. Jane M. Byrne, then Chicago Commissioner of Sales, Weights and Measures,[1] suggested consumers might suffer monetary losses because of the differences in the EPA mileage ratings for the two engines. On the other hand, the federal fuel economy labels pasted on the windows of each Delta 88 carried miles-per-gallon figures for whichever engine was installed in that particular car. Thus, customers inspecting cars on a dealer's lot could expect actual fuel economy to correspond with the window label for any car they were looking at.

Another factor contributing to the GM engine controversy was the practice of labeling engines by divisions regardless of where they were manufactured. Oldsmobile put Rocket stickers on the air cleaners of thousands of its 1977 model cars although the engines were made by Buick or Chevrolet in many cases. Pontiac also labeled some engines with Pontiac symbols even though they were manufactured by other divisions.

The widespread customer reaction to the news that General Motors installed Chevy 350 engines in other lines of cars prompted GM to make a special offer to the owners of these cars in April of 1977. An unhappy owner could return the original car to the dealer for a credit toward the purchase of another 1977 car from the same GM division with whatever engine was then available on the model selected. The credit was based on the purchase price of a car less an 8 cents-a-mile charge for accumulated mileage. Thus, if a car had been driven 4000 miles, the owner would have to pay $320 to trade for the same model. The offer by GM did not assure customers they would get a Buick, Olds, or Pontiac engine in their new car. If a customer turned in an Olds Delta 88 with a Chevy 350 engine, the only way to be sure he or she received a Rocket engine would be to trade up to the higher priced Olds 98 model. Customers who traded for higher priced models would also have to pay additional sales taxes and license fees. Dealers received a credit for $300 for each Chevy powered car traded in to cover their costs of handling the transaction.

Customers who did not want to exchange their cars could accept GM's offer of a free 36 month or 36,000 mile insurance policy on the Chevy engine, transmission, and rear axle. The standard GM new car warranty was for 12 months or 12,000 miles, whichever came first. Customers who traded cars were not eligible for the engine insurance policy. GM's extension of the warranty was apparently a move to reassure owners that the Chevrolet engine would not affect the car's reliability. The exchange and insurance plans were designed to eliminate customer distress over the engine substitutions, and GM President Elliott M. Estes stated, "We are determined . . . to make sure the customer is satisfied with his GM product."[2]

Another apparent goal of the exchange and insurance plans was to encourage Joe Siwek to accept another car so he would withdraw his complaint to the Chicago Consumer Advocate's Office and the Illinois lawsuit could be dismissed. Joe Siwek, however, did not accept GM's offer, contending that he should receive a new engine or a new car at no additional charge. Despite the failure to resolve the Illinois litigation, a number of Detroit observers believed that GM's exchange plan would serve as a pattern for settling many of the lawsuits related to the 350 engine switch. Indeed, after the plan was announced, several states indicated they would halt legal action. General Motors did not intend the exchange offer and the free engine insurance policy to be an admission of guilt in the pending legal actions, but it seemed clear the move was designed to limit the number of cases brought to trial. General Motors did not feel it deceived consumers and said that "when all the facts are presented, we will prevail in the courts."[3]

GM's car exchange offer applied to 81,000 Oldsmobiles, 22,000 Pontiacs, and 25,000 Buicks manufactured before April 10, 1977. About 60,000 customers responded to the GM offer by selecting the free three year insurance plan on the 350 Chevy engine. The fact that only 9,500 of the eligible owners brought in their cars for exchange showed most people were satisfied with the Chevy engine. However, some customers used the offer to take advantage of General Motors. One dealer reported a customer turned in a 1977 Buick Skylark for a 1977 Buick Regal and knowingly took the same 350

Chevy engine. This particular customer just liked the interior of the Regal better than the Skylark.

The estimated cost to General Motors for the car exchange offer and the free three year engine insurance plan was $12 million. This did not include a provision for any legal fees that might arise from the pending lawsuits. In view of these costs and the loss of goodwill, some will argue that GM should have expanded Oldsmobile's capacity to make 350 Rocket engines in 1975 or 1976. The problem with this proposal is that V-8 engines will be phased out of all GM cars by 1985 to meet federal fuel economy standards. Thus, it did not make much sense for GM to expand capacity for Olds V-8 engines at a time when there was a surplus of Chevy 350 engines and V-8's were being discontinued.

In the final analysis, the engine switches made a lot of car buyers angry, and this says something about how consumers react to problems and how General Motors handled the controversy. Although the courts will decide the legal issue of whether GM really deceived customers, one can only speculate on the long-run effects on goodwill, and the nagging question if GM actually lost any money on the sale of the "Chevymobiles."

Appendix A:
Selected Sections from the Illinois Consumer Fraud Act

2. Unfair methods of competition and unfair or deceptive acts or practices, including but not limited to the use or employment of any deception, fraud, false pretense, false promise, misrepresentation or the conceal-ment, suppression or omission of any material fact, with intent that others rely upon the concealment, suppression or omission of such material fact, or the use or employment of any practice described in Sec-tion 2 of the "Uniform Deceptive Trade Practices Act," approved August 5, 1965, in the conduct of any trade or commerce are hereby declared unlawful whether any person has in fact been misled, deceived or dam-aged thereby. In construing this section, consideration shall be given to the interpretations of the Federal Trade Commission and the federal courts relating to Section 5 (a) of the Federal Trade Commission Act.

4. To accomplish the objectives and to carry out the duties prescribed by this Act, the Attorney General, in addition to other powers conferred upon him by this Act, may issue subpoenas to any person, administer an oath of affirmation to any person, conduct hearings in aid of any in-vestigation or inquiry, prescribe such forms and promulgate such rules and regulations as may be necessary, which rules and regulations shall have the force of law.

6. If any person fails or refuses to file any statement or report, or obey any subpoena issued by the Attorney General, the Attorney General may apply to a Circuit Court and, after hearing thereon, request an order:
   a. Granting injunctive relief, restraining the sale or advertisement of any merchandise by such persons, or the conduct of any trade or commerce that is involved;
   b. Vacating, annulling, or suspending the corporate charter of a corporation created by or under the laws of this State or revoking or suspending the certificate of authority to do business in this State of a foreign corporation or revoking or suspending any other licenses, permits, or certificates issued pursuant to law to such person which are used to further the allegedly unlawful practice; and
   c. Granting such other relief as may be required; until the person files the statement or report, or obeys the subpoena.
7. Whenever the Attorney General has reason to believe that any person is using, or has used, or is about to use any method, act, or practice declared by Section 2 of this Act to be unlawful, and that proceedings would be in the public interest, he may bring an action in the name of the State against such person to restrain by temporary or permanent injunction the use of such method, act, or practice. The court, in its discretion, may exercise all equitable powers necessary, including but not limited to: injunction; revocation, forfeiture or suspension of any license, charter, franchise, certificate, or other evidence of authority of any person to do business in this State; appointment of a receiver, dissolution of domestic corporations or associations; suspension or termination of the right of foreign corporations or associations to do business in this State; and restitutiton.

   In addition to the remedies provided herein, the Attorney General may request and this Court has authority to impose a civil penalty in a sum not to exceed $50,000 against any person found by the Court to have engaged in any method, act, or practice declared unlawful under Section 2 of this Act.

Selected Selections from the Illinois Uniform Deceptive Trade Practices Act

2. A person engages in a deceptive trade practice when, in the course of his business, vocation, or occupation, he:
   a. passes off goods or services as those of another;
   b. causes likelihood of confusion or of misunderstanding as to the source, sponsorship, approval, or certification of goods or services;
   c. causes likelihood of confusion or of misunderstanding as to affiliation, connection, or association with a certification by another;

d. uses deceptive representations or designations of geographic origin in connection with goods or services;

e. represents that goods or services have sponsorship, approval, characteristics, ingredients, uses, benefits, or quantities that they do not have or that a person has a sponsorship, approval, status, affiliation or connection that he does not have;

f. represents that goods are original or new if they are deteriorated, altered, reconditioned, reclaimed, used or secondhand;

g. represents that goods or services are a particular standard, quality, or grade or that goods are a particular style or model, if they are of another;

h. disparages the goods, services, or business of another by false or misleading representation of fact;

i. advertises goods or services with intent not to sell them as advertised;

j. advertises goods or services with intent not to supply reasonably expectable public demand, unless the advertisement discloses a limitation of quantity;

k. makes false or misleading statements of fact concerning the reasons for, existence of or amounts of price reductions;

l. engages in any other conduct which similarly creates a likelihood of confusion or of misunderstanding.

In order to prevail in an action under this Act, a plaintiff need prove competition between the parties or actual confusion or misunderstanding.

This Section does not affect unfair trade practices otherwise actionable at common law or under other statutes of this State.

3. A person likely to be damaged by a deceptive trade practice of another may be granted an injunction upon terms that the court considers reasonable. Proof of monetary damage, loss of profits or intent to deceive is not required. Relief granted for the copying of an article shall be limited to the prevention of confusion or misunderstanding as to source.

Costs or attorney's fees or both may be assessed against a defendant only if the court finds that he has willfully engaged in a deceptive trade practice.

The relief provided in this Section is in addition to remedies otherwise available against the same conduct under the common law or other statutes of this State.

Notes

1. Who later became the mayor of Chicago.
2. *Automotive News,* May 2, 1977, p. 8.
3. *Automotive News,* May 2, 1977, p. 2.

Appendix 2C
Giant Food's
Elimination of Item Pricing

One of the areas hardest hit by the recent rapid inflation spiral has been the grocery chain industry. Faced with a sharp rise in the wholesale price index since the 1960s and with mounting pressure from the United Food and Commercial Workers Union for salary increases, the grocery industry began in the late 1960s to explore the possibility of automating its checkout and stocking procedures. The idea of marking each item to be sold with a distinctive label, which would come to be known as the "Universal Product Code" (UPC), had been around since the 1940s. With the development of optical scanning devices and relatively low-cost computers to store and process the information, the idea was becoming increasingly feasible. A joint Ad Hoc Committee of the National Association of Food Chains, the grocery industry's trade association, and the Super Market Institute, the research organization of the industry, met with Distribution Codes, Inc. and representatives of food wholesaler and processor groups to develop the now familiar "zebra code" of ten black and white stripes.

By use of the UPC, groceries can be rung up by passing the bar code label over an optical scanner located at the check stand. There a laser beam "reads" the code through electronic impulses transmitted to the store's computer. The computer in turn looks up the item name and price and sends them to the check stand for electronic display and to its own data files for sales and inventory recordkeeping. For the shopper, it produces an enhanced register tape that describes each item as well as giving the price.

The cost of printing the UPC on containers is small. The capital outlay in installing a checkout system capable of utilizing the UPC is correspondingly attractive. A study made by the Ad Hoc Committee found that in a ten-register store with a projected monthly sales volume of $700,000, the introduction of a UPC system was expected to produce roughly a $10,000 cost savings, or approximately 1.42% of sales.[1] The elimination of placing a price

This case was prepared by Sarah Westrick and revised by Tom L. Beauchamp. © Tom L. Beauchamp. From Tom L. Beauchamp, *Case Studies in Business, Society and Ethics* (Englewood Cliffs, N.J.: Prentice-Hall, Inc., 1983), pp. 82–88. Reprinted with permission.

sticker on each individual item is a significant by-product of the UPC. This factor alone accounts for 0.5% of sales, while the balance would result from increased checkout speed, checkout and marketing accuracy, and routinized restocking. In addition, the data collected by the computer promised major advances in inventory control and pricing; chief among these were reduction of storage time and breakage through direct transfer of merchandise from supplier to shelf and exact turn-over time of shelf stock.

Attracted by this opportunity to hold down operating costs and increase productivity, Giant Food, Inc., a major Maryland-Washington, D.C.-Virginia area grocery chain, began to consider the possibility of installing such a system in a new store. In order to better assess possible problems involved in introducing such novel technology, Giant's consumer advisor, Esther Peterson, organized an advisory committee composed of local consumer group representatives and members of the consumer affairs offices of local governments. Among issues considered by the committee were possible health hazards from the lasers used to read the UPC, improvement of register tape and shelf label formats, employee training, threats to consumer privacy, and the question of discontinuing of item pricing.

The committee's position on this last issue was that consumers had not been exposed to computerized checkout systems long enough for Giant to try experimenting with all aspects of it, and that the abolition of item pricing should be postponed until shoppers were thoroughly familiar with the new system. Concurrently, the United Food and Commercial Workers Union was negotiating a contract with Giant which specified that no employee would be laid off or downgraded if the new system fulfilled all its expected labor-saving functions. Giant, however, was not obligated to replace employees lost to normal attrition from computerized stores if positions became redundant.

Despite a strongly stated policy of consumerism, Giant management chose to override the recommendations of its own advisory group and test the whole system immediately, including the experimental elimination of item pricing.

Before the new computerized store was opened in Severna Park, Maryland in 1975, Giant undertook a series of press conferences and educational measures to familiarize the public with the new system. Booklets were distributed that explained computerized checkout and the UPC, and a demonstration scanner was set up where customers could use it. Radio and TV spots were also used. When the Severna Park store was stocked, unit and item prices (mandatory in Maryland since 1972) were clearly marked on shelf labels, but individual bottles and boxes were not priced.

On opening day shoppers faced a picket line set up by the Maryland Citizens' Consumer Council (MCCC), which distributed leaflets claiming that the removal of item prices was an experiment by Giant to eliminate consumer awareness and leave the shopper at the mercy of the computer. The MCCC was not composed simply of traditionalists opposed to the progress and efficiency introduced by modern technology. They had a number of concerns, all focused on the conditions of consumer ignorance introduced by the new system. For example, computers frequently make mistakes. In order to know at the checkout counter whether a computer was making a mistake, one would have to remember the price of every item (as listed on the shelves) in order to know whether the computer was accurate. The MCCC also argued that it would be much harder for shoppers to follow price increases under the new system. Many shoppers prefer to make comparisons at home by comparing old purchases with new ones. This could now be done only by the tedious and complex process of checking old print-out tapes with new ones. The net effect, consumer groups argued, would be a decreasing awareness of the prices of all grocery store items. A series of concerns of this sort led the MCCC to urge shoppers to voice their complaints directly to the Maryland Legislature, where they found a sympathetic ear. The result was a quick introduction of a bill requiring virtually all groceries to be item priced.

In response to this unexpected attack, the Ad Hoc Committee of the National Association of Food Chains formed a Public Policy Subcommittee (PPS) to dicuss UPC issues. It included Joseph Danzanksy, chairman of Giant Food, Inc., as well as a representative from the National Consumer League and a labor representative from the industry's Joint Labor-Management Committee. The Severna Park store had opened in January 1975; by March the PPS had commissioned a study of the impact of omitting item pricing on consumer awareness and had published a preliminary study of possible industry responses to negative reaction toward price removal.

In the Maryland Senate, hearings were already underway on a mandatory pricing bill. It was agreed, however, to postpone them until February 1976, when the PPS's study would be completed. Meanwhile, due to the proximity of the action to the nation's capital and its resident advocate groups, the issue caught fire with other consumer organizations and the press. By fall of 1975 a bill mandating item pricing had been introduced in the U.S. Senate.

Meanwhile Giant had been collecting comment cards from its Severna Park store in order to conduct its own assessment of consumer reaction. Opinions represented by the first two months of responses stayed essentially the same throughout the year: 86.5% of shoppers liked the system; 7.8% disliked it; and 5.7% were undecided. 24.7% of all those surveyed still wanted item pricing. In August 1975 Giant had opened a second computerized store in the neighboring town of Glen Burnie, Maryland. In accordance with a promise made after the opening of the Severna Park store to retain item pricing in all other stores until a policy could be made, the Glen Burnie store used the UPC system but retained individually priced items. There it was found, in comparison with the figures from Severna Park, that while 93% of the shoppers liked the system, 32% wanted to keep individual pricing.

Shortly after the opening of Severna Park, in a speech before the Super Market Institute, Mr. Danzansky said:

> There are those who maintain that [the food retailer] is but an extension of the chain of food production, processing and manufacturing. I am among those who believe that the food retailer's function is to serve as the purchasing agent for the customer. The customer is no longer in a position to assess market conditions. . . . It is up to us to be sure that we, on [the customer's] behalf, purchase good products at the best prices and give [the customer] the information [needed] to buy intelligently.[2]

In November, before the Subcommittee on the Consumer of the U.S. Senate Commerce Committee, Danzanksy urged the Subcommittee to give an unfavorable report on the mandatory pricing bill, arguing that unfavorable reaction was the result of ignorance and fear of novelty. He stressed that Giant had not yet decided what policy to follow in regard to item pricing and stated that the ultimate decision should come from the shoppers. He added that "the government (by aborting Giant's experiment with item price removal) should not deprive the consumer of the right to make that decision."[3] A few weeks later he was echoed by Mrs. Peterson:

> There is no room for debate on whether or not consumers have the right to be informed at the point of purchase about the prices they are paying for items. This is a basic right. . . . I do not believe, however, that we have legislated nor can we effectively legislate the specific manner in which this is done.[4]

In February 1976 they both testified against mandatory item pricing legislation before the Maryland House of Delegates. It was reported then that Giant's actual savings from use of the UPC without item pricing at the Severna Park store amounted to two percent of sales, 11% above the savings that had been anticipated.[5]

Six weeks later the Maryland House passed a mandatory pricemarking bill. Three days thereafter, the Ad Hoc Committee's Public Policy Subcommittee released its study of consumer price awareness in the absence of item pricing. This study had been performed in matching stores, with and without individually priced items. It showed that some shoppers in the stores that omitted the price from individual items did indeed experience significant loss of price awareness. In an accompanying policy statement the Subcommittee said:

> The Public Policy Subcommittee is recommending to the industry that scanner stores follow the same traditional approach to individual itemmarking as is used in conventional supermarkets. . . .
>
> The Subcommittee believes that creating and maintaining consumer price awareness, while lowering the cost of food, are worthy and complex

goals. The concepts and techniques of attaining these goals are far from resolved.[6]

Giant later announced that it would act on the Subcommittee's recommendation; Giant introduced item pricing to the Severna Park store and retained it in all existing and new stores.

In response, the Maryland Senate allowed the mandatory pricing bill to die. The following fall, the United Food and Commercial Workers Union ceased lobbying for item pricing on Capitol Hill, and there too mandatory pricing legislation was dropped. During the 14 months of Giant's experiment at Severna Park, four states—Massachusetts, Rhode Island, Connecticut, and California—had witnessed the successful enactment of mandatory pricing bills, either on the state or local level. Of the 28 states with pending legislation, only two more—New York and Michigan—passed their bills. Local ordinances in Florida were subsequently passed that required individual items to be priced, but no legislation affecting Giant ever passed. Meanwhile the UPC was so universally adopted by the food processing industry that 95–98% of all items came to bear the bar code.

In 1978 Giant had 36 stores using the scanning system and a resulting large data base from which to assess the effectiveness of the UPC system. Giant found that in a store grossing $700,000 monthly, the savings brought about by computer-assisted checkout were $6,634, or slightly less than one percent of sales. This was 50% less than the savings experienced at Severna Park when item pricing had been omitted.

Giant subsequently opened a new store in Clinton, Maryland in October 1980. In this store cases of merchandise were set out directly on the shelves, with top and sides removed. While not a so-called "warehouse" store, the number of brands and package sizes available were significantly reduced (up to 50% of the usual selection). To the consternation of the Consumer's Right to Information Committee (CRIC)—a group originally composed of national and local consumer groups and local labor—the individual cans and boxes were not priced and Giant announced plans to continue the practice in its next three stores, scheduled to be opened within a few weeks. After meeting with Giant officials, CRIC expressed deep concern over this renewed threat to consumer price awareness. Giant's answer implied that the new system, including improved shelf labels and lower prices, would help shoppers and would lower their food bills.

The Economic Affairs Committee of the Maryland Senate was not pleased by the news of Giant's efforts. Joseph Danzansky had promised at the time Giant had agreed to follow the PPS's recommendation on item pricing that he would consult with the Committee if Giant should ever reconsider removing item prices. Mr. Danzansky died in 1979, however, and the present Giant officials had failed to communicate their intentions to the Committee. Backed by the Consumer's Right to Information Committee, the senators expressed their displeasure by introducing a bill requiring price tags on all items sold in the state. Local 400 of the United Food and Commercial Workers declined to take a position on the bill, stating only that Giant had failed to show how discontinuation of item pricing would result in labor reductions significant enough to create job losses. The bill ultimately expired.

In April 1981 Giant announced that due to the successful operation of its "no-frills" stores, it was instituting substantially decreased "warehouse prices" on 1,500 to 2,000 items, about 17% of its stock, in *all* its stores. These price reductions would be made possible, Giant officials said, by dropping item pricing entirely—thus producing savings in the labor costs of marking each item individually. Giant did not plan to stop marking prices on all items immediately, but as new stock was placed on the shelves the program would gradually be expanded to include all merchandise. A study done by *Food World*, a publication doing market-share surveys of the grocery industry, showed that during the month of April 1981, Giant's sales increased about 14%, bringing its percentage of the Washington area grocery dollar to $.34 or 7% over Safeway, a national chain and Giant's closest competitor.[7]

While Giant's lowered prices actually resulted in a net loss during the second half of 1981, the demand for scanning systems increased 168% during an 18-month period ending in August 1981, according to *Business Week*. Nearly 4,000 of an estimated 33,000 supermarkets in the United States and Canada employed them by mid-1981.[8] Giant's example and consumer reaction have been watched closely in Washington, where interest has increased markedly among other stores in the Washington-Maryland-Virginia area. In early 1982 twenty of the 125 Safeway stores in the area had scanning systems, and the chain had an additional 48 stores with "intelligent" registers, which are less sophisticated than the computer-linked registers used by Giant. Safeway adopted a no-prices policy in all stores equipped with scanners and hoped to install some type of scanning system in most of its stores as quickly as possible. Giant's customer counts and total sales never decreased throughout the entire period, and in fact showed a steady increase.[9]

Notes

1. These and other figures given by the Ad Hoc Commitee or quoted by Giant representatives, unless otherwise noted, are taken from: "Giant Food and the Universal Product Code," in Earl A. Molander, *Responsive Capitalism: Case Studies in Corporate Social Conduct* (New York: McGraw-Hill, 1980), pp. 100–112.

2. Speech given to the Super Market Institute, Washington, D.C., February 28, 1976, p.1.

3. *Hearings before the Subcommittee on the Consumer, U.S. Senate Committee on Commerce, on S.997,* "Amending the Fair Packaging and Labeling Act," November 3, 1975, p. 8 of Joseph Danzansky's testimony.

4. Ibid., November 17, 1975, p. 1 of Esther Peterson's testimony.

5. *Hearings before the Maryland Senate, Economic Affairs Committee, on S. 100,* "Pricing of Consumer Commodities," February 2, 1978, p. 3 of Joseph Danzansky's testimony.

6. Public Policy Subcommittee of the Ad Hoc Committee on the Universal Product Code, *Policy Statement on Item Pricing* (Washington, D.C., March 23, 1976), p. 2.

7. *Washington Post,* "Shelf Pricing May Help Giant Food Win Cost War," May 10, 1981, sec. 1, p. 1.

8. *Business Week,* "Supermarket Scanners Get Smarter" (August 17, 1981), p. 88.

9. According to Mr. Barry F. Scher, Director of Public Affairs for Giant. Private correspondence of April 1, 1982.

Appendix 2D
The Marketing of Infant Formula in Less Developed Countries

S. Prakash Sethi
James E. Post

T he activities of multinational corporations (MNCs) in less developed countries (LDCs) have been justified on many grounds. The foremost among the benefits accruing to the less developed countries are the transfer of superior technology and management skills; the creation of jobs and of a broader economic base, and so, an improved standard of living; and the provision of superior goods at reasonable prices. These benefits are possible because multinational companies operate from a large base of resources, thereby exploiting economies of scale; and because MNC research and development facilities ensure superior products through in-house testing and quality control. The last point is quite critical in the case of a variety of products and services. The consumers in LDCs usually do not have either the information or necessary skills to evaluate the multitude of new products that are introduced by the MNCs. These products are quite often outside their cultural frame of reference, and so evaluation through comparisons with local products is not possible.

The small size of total demand makes it unattractive for more than one or two companies to compete for the market. Thus the role of competition in disciplining the suppliers and providing the consumers with necessary comparative information is limited. The LDCs are generally deficient in institutional mechanisms for inspection and regulation that would ensure the production and sale of products in a manner that serves public interest while also ensuring reasonable profits to the MNCs.

Dimension of the Problem

At the aggregate level, the assumption that MNCs serve public interest in host countries through their activities in the private sector is largely support-

© 1979 by the Regents of the University of California. Condensed from *California Management Review*, volume XXI, no. 4, pp. 35–48, by permission of the Regents.

able. However, at the level of the single company or industry in the single country, this is not necessarily so. Therefore, while a MNC may not have deliberately violated any laws, its normal activities in pursuit of self-interest may have untoward social consequences. All marketing activities of individual firms have second order effects that extend far beyond the boundaries of the parties to the immediate exchange. Quite often, these effects are far more pervasive in their collectivity than visualized by individual firms when making simple transactions. While the users of the product or those indirectly affected by it are unable to seek adequate remedy and relief in the market place, the cumulative effect of their dissatisfactions results in transferring the issue from the private to public domain.

This article focuses on a study of the infant formula foods by large MNCs in less developed countries to demonstrate the nature of second order effects of primary activities, the promotion and sale of infant formula foods. The basic questions raised are:

> To what extent should a firm be responsible for the undirected use of its products? Ought not the demand for a product the marketing of which is legal be the ultimate count in the MNC's decision to undertake its manufacture and sale?

> Under what circumstances should a corporation exercise self-restraint in advertising? Does the corporation have an obligation to promote only those products which it knows will be used correctly? Should a competitor's successful manufacture and promotion of a product influence a company to enter the market and utilize similar tactics?

> The operation of the market economies assures that the second order effects of a firm's activities are in the public domain and so must be handled by government agencies, leaving individual firms to pursue their self-interest unfettered by external considerations. Is it feasible or desirable for a MNC to assume a posture that is primarily market-oriented? What role can the LDC government be expected to play in this area? Should there be a government-directed choice of products a private corporation could manufacture? Finally, once a private market-oriented issue gets into the public domain, what changes should MNCs make to assuage society's demands?

Infant Formula Foods: The Industry[1]

Infant formula food was developed in the early 1920s as an alternative to breast-feeding. Sales rose sharply after World War II, and hit a peak in the late 1950s, following the 4.3 million births in 1957.[2] However, birth rates began declining in the 1960s, and by 1974 the annual number of births had declined to 3.1 million. The low birth rate caused a steep downturn in baby formula food sales.

The major U.S. and foreign companies engaged in the manufacture and marketing of infant formulas include Abbott Laboratories, which produces *Similac* and *Isomil* infant formulas through its Ross Laboratories division; American Home Products, which produces *SMA, S26,* and *Nursoy* infant formulas through its Wyeth Laboratories; Bristol-Myers, which produces *Enfamil, Olac,* and *Prosobee* through its Mead Johnson Division; Nestlé Alimentana, S.A., a Swiss multinational; and Unigate, a British firm. In their search for business, these companies began developing markets in third world countries, where population was still expanding, while baby food markets in developed countries were leveling off.

The international market for infant formula grew rapidly during the post–World War II era. Although a number of food companies had sold breast-milk substitutes in western Europe before that time, many of these products, made of evaporated milk or powdered milk, were not nutritionally equivalent to human milk, as are formulas. As prosperity returned to Europe and multinational firms expanded operations in Africa, South America and the Far East, infant formula became the "food of choice" for the children of expatriate Americans and western Europeans.

The large number of wealthy and middle-class persons able to afford infant formula in the U.S. and Europe made mass distribution and promotion of such products a widespread and acceptable phenomenon. In Africa, South America, and the Far East, however, the number of wealthy customers was fewer, and the size of the middle class was notably smaller. Local distributors were often used as a means of distributing the product. In an effort to expand sales, distributors, and sometimes the manufacturers themselves, began to promote the infant formula to broad segments of the population. This promotion reached the poor and those only marginally able to afford the product in less developed nations and produced the infant formula controversy.

Business Strategy

After intense competitive battles, Ross Laboratories and Mead Johnson emerged as the winners in the United States market. By the 1960s, the two firms commanded approximately 90 percent of the domestic infant formula business (Ross's *Similac* 55 percent, Mead Johnson's *Enfamil* about 35 percent). So entrenched were these sellers in the domestic market that Nestlé, the acknowledged worldwide industry leader with 50 percent of the market, never attempted to penetrate the U.S. market.

With the leveling off in the U.S. birth rate in the 1960s, both Ross and Mead Johnson began to look outside the U.S. for major growth opportunities. This effort led Ross to industrialized nations with higher disposable income and prospects for market penetration. Canada and Europe became major foreign markets for Ross's *Similac*. Mead Johnson looked primarily to the Caribbean where export was relatively easy. Puerto Rico, Jamaica, and the Bahamas became important Mead Johnson export markets.

Wyeth Laboratories, never a major seller of infant formula in the United States, began to sell internationally before World War II. Following the war, the company's presence as a pharmaceutical manufacturer was the base from which infant formula was marketed by affiliates in Latin America, Europe, and Southeast Asia. Today, Wyeth probably accounts for close to 15 percent of worldwide sales.

Growth in Infant Formula Sales in LDCs

Studies point to an increasing trend toward bottle-feeding in LDCs. In developing nations, breast-feeding has declined substantially and the length of the nursing period has shrunk from over a year to a few months.

Three important environmental factors[3] account for the shift toward bottle-feeding in LDCs. These are the sociocultural changes in developing countries, the changing attitudes of health workers and health institutions, and the promotional activities of infant formula manufacturers.

The sociocultural factors influencing change in infant feeding can be understood primarily in terms of urbanization, which has caused the westernization of social mores and the need for mobility in employment. High income groups were the first to use infant formula, in imitation of western practices, and thus bottle-feeding came to represent a high-status modern practice. Low income groups tended to follow suit. Too, the breast has come to be viewed as a sex symbol, which has led to embarrassment in using it for nursing, and fear that nursing will make the appearance of the breast less desirable. Finally, there is the convenience aspect: most places of employment do not provide facilities for a nursing woman, so bottle-feeding of the infant may become a necessity for a working woman.

Health professionals—doctors, nurses, and clinic workers—and the policies of the hospitals and clinics often, wittingly or unwittingly, endorse the use of infant formula. Although much of this activity originates in the promotional efforts by baby food formula manufacturers to the mother, the endorsement may appear to come from the health professionals themselves. Nurses and social workers who staff hospitals and clinics may encourage the use of bottle-feeding. In many hospitals newborn babies are routinely bottle-fed whether or not the mother plans to breast-feed later. Hospitals and clinics receive free samples of infant milk and special plastic milk bottles which nurses distribute to mothers. These nurses may also distribute "vaccination cards" which advertise infant formulas, and baby care booklets which recommend bottle-feeding.

Industry Promotion Practices

Many observers claim that the infant formula industry's promotion is overly aggressive and has contributed to the decline of breast-feeding. The industry itself, however, feels that its promotion is generally responsible and performs a valuable function. Individual companies have concentrated on different promotional mixes, based on their orientation, i.e., pharmaceutical vs. processed foods; or depending on their market strategies, i.e., maintaining a dominant market position and protecting market share, or getting entry into new markets and increasing market share. Yet their impact from the public interest point of view is not very dissimilar. These practices can be summarized in the following categories.

Baby Food Booklets

One of the major forms of promotion used by baby food companies is the information booklet. Some typical titles are *The Ostermilk Mother and Baby Book: Caring for Your Baby,* published by Ross Laboratories, and *A Life Begins,* published by Nestlé. These booklets are distributed free in maternity wards of public hospitals, clinics, doctors' offices, and by nurses. They provide information on prenatal and postnatal care, with special emphasis given to how babies should be fed. Many of these books are directed to illiterate or semiliterate women, using pictures to show correct or incorrect feeding methods.

Some baby food booklets, usually pre-1975 versions, describe and illustrate bottle-feeding without mentioning breast-feeding. However, as public concern rose over the possible harmful effects of bottle-feeding, promotional booklets began to discuss breast-feeding and to recommend "mixed feeding," in which the bottle is used as a supplement to breast milk. Examples of this type include Nestlé's *Your Baby and You,* which suggests "an occasional bottle-feed . . . if you cannot breast-feed Baby entirely yourself."[4] A Mead Johnson pamphlet states, "More babies have thrived on Mead Johnson formula products than on any other form of supplementary feeding." Cow & Gate recommends its milk to "be used as a substitute for breast-feeding or as a supplement."[5]

In discussing the use of supplements for feeding the baby, these booklets often emphasize reasons to discontinue or diminish breast-feeding. Nestlé, for example, in *A Life Begins,* asserts that bottle-feeding must be substituted for breast-feeding if the mother is ill, if her milk is insufficient for the baby or of "poor quality," or if the mother's nipples crack or become infected. These booklets also suggest that breast-feeding should be diminished to include solid food into the baby's diet. *The Ostermilk Mother and Baby Book* advises introducing solid foods for babies a few weeks old or even earlier, while

Cow & Gate suggests feeding its brand of cereal to the baby from two to three months.[6]

Other Media Practices

Companies did promote their baby food products by advertising in magazines, newspapers, radio, television, and through loudspeaker vans. As with the baby care booklets, early advertisements usually did not mention breast-feeding: a magazine advertisement stated that Ostermilk and Farex products were "right from the start—the foods that you can trust." Poster advertisements, often exhibited in hospitals and clinics, showed how to prepare baby formula, but gave only minimal attention to breast-feeding. Radio and television ads similarly emphasized bottle-feeding.

Free Samples and Gifts

One of the most widespread promotional techniques is the distribution of free samples, and the offer of free gifts to users or potential users of baby food formula. These usually take the form of samples of formula or free feeding bottles, and may be handed out by nurses and salesmen at hospitals, clinics, or in the home. A survey in Ibadan, Nigeria, found that 9 percent of the mothers surveyed had received samples. These had been given in equal proportion to more affluent mothers and to those who could not afford baby food formula. A spokesman from Nestlé admitted that sampling in the Philippines cost about 4–5 percent of turnover.[7] Free gifts are less often used as an inducement to buy.

Promotion through the Medical Profession

Hospitals and physicians are a logical focus for promotion and sales-related advertising. The users of artificial feeding products are sensitive to the "scientific" quality of infant formula, and physicians were the appropriate counselors to give advice. Also, hospitals are becoming increasingly popular as the site for birth, and the newborns are typically fed at the hospital for the first few days of their lives. The decision a new mother makes before birth to feed her child "Brand X" formula could be changed by the hospital's decision to feed infants "Brand Y" or the physician's recommendation to feed "Brand Z." As a marketing matter, prebirth advertising can create consumer awareness of a product; it cannot create sales. Sales creation occurs in the physician's office or in the hospital. For these reasons, the medical community has become the focal point for infant formula promotion in industrialized and developing nations alike.

In general, all promotional methods such as booklets, free samples, posters, and the use of salespeople are employed in the hospitals and clinics. In addition, the use of "milk nurses" and "milk banks" functions to associate baby food formula with the medical profession. "Mother-craft" or milk nurses are fully or partially trained nurses hired by infant food formula companies, and instructed by them in "product knowledge." Most nurses are paid fixed salaries plus a travel allowance, but some may receive sales-related bonuses. A number of hospitals allow milk nurses to speak to mothers in maternity wards or clinics. Nurses visit mothers in their homes, and in some isolated areas, the milk nurses make formula deliveries. A 1974 study conducted by the Caribbean Food and Nutrition Institute found that Mead Johnson, subsidiaries of Nestlé, Glaxo, Ross Laboratories, and Cow & Gate all employed milk nurses in Jamaica. Mead Johnson employed twelve.[8]

Milk banks, usually set up in the hospitals and clinics that serve the poor, are sales outlets for commercial infant food formula. These banks sell formula at reduced prices to poor mothers. For example, at the milk bank at Robert Reid Cabral hospital in Santo Domingo, a pound tin of Nestlés *Nido* is sold for 90¢, a 40 percent discount off the regular $1.50 price; Nestlé's *Nan* is sold for $1.35, a 33 percent discount off the regular price of $2.00

Criticism of Industry Promotion Practices

All forms of promotion used by infant formula companies have been criticized by different observers. In general, critics claim that most forms of advertising are misleading or use "hard sell" techniques to turn mothers away from breast-feeding.

Baby Care Booklets

The main criticism of baby care booklets is that they ignore or de-emphasize breast-feeding. Critics feel that mothers reading these baby care booklets will be led to believe that bottle-feeding is as good as or better than breast-feeding. Even if the booklet directly states "Breast-feeding is best," critics assert that the overall impression is still misleading. The new trend in these books toward promoting "mixed feeding," or the early introduction of solid food is also questioned. The La Leche League International, an organization which promotes breast-feeding observed that:

> . . . the supplementary formula is one of the greatest deterrents to establishing a good milk supply, and frequent nursing is one of the greatest helps. You see, the milk supply is regulated by what the baby takes. The more he nurses, the more milk there will be. If he's given a bottle as well, he'll gradually take less and less from the breast, and the supply will diminish.[9]

In addition, the use of a bottle and overdiluted formula, even as a supplement, can cause infection and malnutrition in the infant.

Promotion through Media

The critics' objections to other media promotion is similar to their objections to the baby care booklets. They feel that even with the admission of the superiority of breast milk, media promotion remains essentially misleading in its encouragement of mothers to bottle-feed their children. A survey in infant feeding practices in Ibadan, Nigeria, revealed that of the 38 percent of 400 mothers who remembered having seen ads for formula, the majority recalled statements to the effect that the formula gives infants strength, energy, and power. None remembered having heard that breast milk is better for babies. In Nigeria, when ads for Ovaltine included the picture of a plump smiling baby, observers noted that there was a trend for mothers to feed their babies Ovaltine and water as a supplement.[10] This misinterpretation of ads is an obvious danger in a predominantly illiterate or semiliterate community.

Free Samples and Gifts

Free samples of baby food formula and feeding bottles, as well as gift gimmicks, are considered a direct inducement to bottle-feed infants. The widespread distribution of these items shows an unethical lack of concern for either informing mothers about the superiority of breast-feeding or for determining whether mothers have the economic ability to regularly buy infant formula after the first samples.

Promotion through the Medical Profession

Critics find the promotion of infant formula through the distribution of free samples and literature or the display of advertising posters in hospitals and clinics especially dangerous. Dr. D.B. Jelliffe, head of the Division of Population, Family, and International Health at UCLA, called these promotional techniques "endorsement by association" and "manipulation by assistance." Jelliffe, along with many other critics, feels that companies providing hospitals and clinics with free samples and information on new developments in infant formula, as well as a barrage of advertisements, influence health care workers to favor and promote bottle-feeding to their patients. It is also argued that because mothers see posters and receive informational booklets and free samples at hospitals and clinics, they come to believe that the health profession endorses bottle-feeding. Thus, this type of promotion works two ways in influencing both the beliefs of professionals and the beliefs of mothers about the value of bottle-feeding.

The use of milk nurses also receives its share of criticism. Observers charge that the nurse uniform conceals the fact that the "nurses" are essentially salespeople who encourage mothers to bottle-feed. They assert that some nurses are paid on a sales-related basis, causing them to be even more eager to push for sales. In support of this belief, critics quote an industry man: "Some nurses will be paid a commission on sales results in their area. Sometimes they will also be given the added stick that if they don't meet those objectives, they will be fired."[11]

Milk Banks

Milk banks are used by companies to expand sales by encouraging bottle-feeding among the poor while still retaining the higher-income market. However, critics assert that the discount prices of the formula are still beyond the economic means of the people at whom the milk banks aim their services. For example, a milk bank in Guatemala City sells Nestlé products for $1.00 per tin, a discount of 80¢ to $1.00 from the regular price. A tin lasts only a few days when properly prepared. However, since the women buying milk there generally have household incomes of between $15 and $45 per month, they commonly buy fewer tins and dilute them. This starts the baby on a cycle of malnutrition and disease.

The Infant Formula Controversy

The first criticism of the industry and its promotional activities is traceable to the late 1960s when Dr. Jelliffe, Director of the Caribbean Food and Nutrition Institute in Jamaica, conducted his research. His findings and criticism culminated in an international conference of experts held in Bogota, Columbia, in 1970, under the auspices of the U.N.'s Protein Calorie Advisory Group (PAG). Out of this meeting, and the 1972 follow-up session in Singapore, came increased professional concern about the effects of commercial activity related to infant feeding. The PAG issued an official statement (PAG, Statement #23) in 1973 recommending that breast-feeding be supported and promoted in LDCs, and that commercial promotion by industry or LDC governments be restrained.

The first public identification of the issue occurred in 1973 with the appearance of several articles about the problem in *The New Internationalist*.[12] This, in turn, spurred Mike Muller to undertake a series of interviews and observations which were eventually printed as *The Baby Killer,* a pamphlet published in 1974.[13] The popularization of the issue resulted in a German translation of Muller's work published in Switzerland under the title, *Nestle Tötet Kinder* (Nestlé Kills Babies); and in a lawsuit by Nestlé against the public action group that published the pamphlet. A period of intense advocacy issued from the trial in the Swiss courts. Thus, between 1974 and mid-1976 when the case was decided, considerable international media coverage was given the issue.

The pressure began in earnest in 1975 when shareholder resolutions were filed for consideration at the annual meetings of the American infant formula companies. This pressure has continued, and several institutional investors such as universities and the Rockefeller and Ford Foundations have taken public positions which sharply question the responsiveness of the firms to the controversy. Church groups have led the fight, and have developed their own institutional mechanism through the National Council of Churches, the Interfaith Council on Corporate Responsibility, to coordinate shareholders' campaigns. At the LDC level, the government of Papua New Guinea recently passed a law declaring that baby bottles, nipples and pacifiers are health hazards, and their sale has been restricted to prescription only. The objective was to discourage indiscriminate promotion, sale and consumption of infant food formulas.[14]

Recently, institutions have acted to broaden their popular base by launching a grass roots campaign to boycott Nestlé products in the United States. By linking public action groups throughout the U.S., the current campaign aspires to heighten First World pressure against the Third World's largest seller of infant formula foods.

Manufacturer Responses

The preproblem stage of the infant formula case existed prior to the 1970s. During this time, the adverse impacts on LDCs were not yet articulated. The MNC's response was of social obligation type, answering only to prevailing law and market conditions. In effect, MNCs were free to conduct their business in ways most consistent with their own orientations and business strategies.

By the early 1970s the identification stage had been reached, as professional criticism grew and articles and stores began to appear in mass media. The principal industry response to this professional concern was participation in the conference sponsored by PAG. Abbott (Ross), AHP (Wyeth), and Nestlé each sent representatives to these meetings as did a number of British, European, and Japanese companies. For most companies, this seemed to mark a decision point between what could be characterized as social obligation and social responsibility. Only a few firms, notably Abbott (Ross), took steps to mitigate their negative impact in the LDCs. AHP (Wyeth), Borden, Nestlé and others did not follow suit until 1974, when first plans for the formation of an international trade organization were laid.

The remedy and relief stage seems to have begun in 1975, with the Nestlé trial in Switzerland and the shareholder resolutions filed in the United States.

In November 1975, representatives of nine MNC manufacturers met in Zurich and formed the International Council of Infant Food Industries (ICIFI). Nestlé, AHP (Wyeth), and Abbott (Ross) participated in these discussions along with several European and four Japanese companies. Others, such as Borden and Bristol-Myers, sent representatives to the sessions, but chose not to participate actively or to join the council. ICIFI's initial directive was to instruct members to adopt a code of marketing ethics which obliged them to recognize the primacy of breast-feeding in all product information and labelling; to include precise product-use information; and to eliminate in-hospital promotion and solicitation by personnel who were paid on a sales-commission basis. For those companies that joined, the council seemed to mark a passage into social responsibility as efforts were undertaken to mitigate negative social impacts.

There was criticism of the ICIFI code from the beginning, and Abbott (Ross) withdrew from the organization, arguing that the code was too weak. The company then adopted its own more restrictive code, which included a provision prohibiting consumer-oriented mass advertising. For ICIFI, the marketing code has been the most visible manifestation of concern for second-order impacts in LDCs. Additional criticism led to some incremental changes which strengthened the "professional" character of sales activity, but which have not yet proscribed all consumer-oriented mass advertising. Thus, ICIFI, the industry's mechanism for countering criticism and searching for means of addressing problems of product misuse in LDC environments, has been unable to reckon with any but the individual-level secondary impacts. Indeed, the critics continue to charge that the response at the user level has been insufficient.

Borden also moved from the social obligation to social responsibility stage. The company had shareholder resolutions filed with it in 1977. This filing perhaps facilitated a management review of promotional strategies in LDCs. In settling the resolution with the church groups before the meeting, Borden agreed to modify certain advertising and labelling of its powdered milk *Klim*; and to tightly oversee the marketing so as to minimize possible consumer misuse of the powdered milk product as an infant formula food. Separately, the company announced that it was withdrawing its infant formula *New Biolac* from two LDC markets in the Far East because it concluded it could not effectively market this product without extensive consumer advertising which was not permissible in the prevailing social-political environment.

As a public issue matures, companies may adopt actions which operate to prevent further growth in the legitimacy gap by minimizing or eliminating the underlying sources of criticism (a prevention stage). This has begun to occur in the infant formula controversy as both ICIFI and individual companies have taken action to prevent some of the secondary impacts discussed above. In 1977, Abbott (Ross) announced its intention to commit nearly $100,000 to a breast-feeding campaign in developing nations, and to budget $175,000 for a task force to conduct research on breast-feeding, infant formula, and LDCs. The company also announced a plan for a continuing cooperative effort with its critics in reviewing the situation. ICIFI has now also gone beyond its marketing code of ethics and has begun informally working with international health agencies to prepare educational materials, for use in LDCs, that would encourage breast-feeding and improve maternal and infant health care. The council is also involved in supporting scientific research of breast-feeding, infant formula products, and LDC environments.

Abbott (Ross) Laboratories' attempt to act in a way that will create positive impacts in LDCs signals a shift to a corporate social responsiveness. Granting that there is some danger of sending "double signals" to its sales force, the company seems to have adopted a posture that permits the sale of its products in appropriate circumstances, and assists the LDCs in encouraging breast-feeding where that is most appropriate.

Conclusion

The manner in which all organizations, particularly large corporations, respond to social change is a matter of great public concern. Their economic actions necessarily involve social changes and may have such an impact on established behavioral patterns and underlying cultural values and beliefs as to cause tremendous social stress. This is especially true in the case of LDCs. There is reason to believe that the effect of the modern corporation is even more profound in social and economic settings where there are fewer countervailing influences than exist in industrialized societies. These nations are in the process of becoming modernized and there is tension between the values of the old and the new, the technology of the past and the future, and the aspirations of the present with the traditions of the past. The modern corporation generally represents the new and the future. In such situations, it is not surprising that the impact of the corporation concerns those who care about the pace, the process, and the direction of development and change.

Infant nutrition is one area in which the complex interaction of changing social values, institutions, and technology has produced major changes in social habits. According to many public health and nutrition experts, there now exists a crisis of monumental proportions in LDCs as mothers abandon traditional breast-feeding practices in favor of bottle-feeding. In the view of some critics, the bottle has become a symbol of the most invidious intrusion of western technology into the lives and welfare of LDC populations. One might fairly conclude that the "great infant formula controversy" is one involving the politics of technology.

The objectives of MNCs and LDCs are not always congruent with each other. Nevertheless, there must be a common ground where the interaction between the two yields net benefits, both tangible and intangible, if any sustained cooperation is to take place. Conventional economic analysis shows direct costs and benefits of individual MNC-LDC cooperation, but usually overlooks social and political costs. These costs are difficult to calculate, as there is no common consensus of what they are or how they might be measured; and there is a fear that if these costs were specified, they could doom MNC projects. The cultural and sociopolitical costs are of critical importance. The long-range social acceptance on the part of the peoples in LDCs of MNC's investments depends on the decisions of MNC and LDC governments to taking these costs into account when developing economic projects.

Notes

1. Much of this material comes from James E. Post, testimony in *Marketing and Promotion of Infant Formula in the Developing Nations,* Hearings before the Subcommittee on Health and Scientific Research of the Committee on Human Resources, 95th Congress, Second Session, 23 May 1978, pp. 116–125.

2. Robert J. Ledogar, *U.S. Food and Drug Multinationals in Latin America: Hungry for Profits* (New York: IDOC, North America, Inc., 1975), p. 128.

3. Johanna T. Dwyer, "The Demise of Breast Feeding: Sales, Sloth, or Society?" in *Priorities in Child Nutrition,* report prepared for the UNICEF Executive Board under the direction of Dr. Jean Mayer (E/ICEF/L. 1328, March 28, 1975), vol. II, pp. 332–339.

4. Ledogar, op. cit., pp. 133–134.

5. Ibid.

6. Ibid., p. 142.

7. Frances M. Lappé and Eleanor McCallie, "Infant Formula Promotion and Use in the Philippines: An Informal, On-Site Report," Institute for Food and Development Policy (San Francisco, California, July 1977). Lappé is the author of the new book, *Food First.*

8. V.G. James, "Household Expenditures on Food and Drink by Income Groups," paper presented at seminar on Natural Food and Nutrition Policy, Kingston, Jamaica, 1974.

9. *The Womanly Art of Breastfeeding,* 2nd ed. (Franklin Park, Ill.: La Leche League International, 1963), p. 54.

10. "Baby Food Tragedy," *New Internationalist,* p. 10; Mike Muller, *The Baby Killer: War on Want,* 2nd ed. (May 1975), p. 10.

11. Bristol-Myers Co., "The Infant Formula Marketing Practices," p. 13.

12. "The Baby Food Controversy," *New Internationalist,* p. 10.

13. Muller, op. cit.

14. "Baby Bottles Banned in New Guinea," *The Dallas Morning News* (November 3, 1977), p. 8-C.

Index

Advertising ethics, 27–40, 129–133;
  code of, 133. *See also* Puffery;
  Manipulation in advertising
Alderson, Wroe, 12
American Assembly of Collegiate
  Schools of Business (AACSB), 7,
  104
American Heart Association, 33
American Marketing Association, xv,
  33, 57, 58, 64, 65, 101
Antitrust law, 75
Arrington, Robert L., 32, 39
AT&T, 102
Austin, Robert W., 75

Baksheesh, 86
Bartels, Robert, 12, 71
Baumhart, Raymond C., 5, 105
Beach, F.H., 42
Beauchamp, Tom L., 14, 74
Becker, Helmut, 86
Bell, Martin L., 76
Benson, George, 74
Berkman, H.W., 43
Berkowitz, E.N., 42–43, 49, 71, 74
Birnhaum, T., 35
Bogart, L., 59, 62, 67
Boling, T.E., 43
Boulding, Kenneth, 33
Bowie, Norman, 14, 44, 73–74
Boyd, H.W., 47
Brenner, S.N., 43
Bribery, 122–124. *See also* Foreign
  Corrupt Practices Act
Brien, R.H., 55
Bronson, Gail, 35
Buchholz, R.A., 9, 43, 71, 78

Buckner, Robert, 91
Business ethics courses, 6
Business Roundtable, 77
Buskirk, R.H., 42

Carlson, R.O., 56
Carol, Archie B., 97
Categorical imperative, 88
Caterpillar, code of ethics, 37–38, 77
Caterpillar Tractor Company, 37, 77,
  111–116
Cavenaugh, Gerald F., 93
Celanese Corporation, 86
Chivas Regal, 29, 32
Churchill, G.A., 42, 47–48
Clasen, Earl A., 77
Clinard, Raymond C., 3–5
Cocanougher, A. Benton, 9, 55, 71,
  100
Codes of conduct, 37–38, 100–102;
  examples of, 107–136; for market-
  ing research, 58; for pricing, 81;
  problems with, 101
Colihan, William J., 12
Common Market, 86, 90
Conflict of interest, 136
Consoli, John, 35
Continental Grain Corporation, 91–92
Corporate espionage, 68, 120–122
Council on Environmental Quality, 85
Crawford, C.M., 56
Cultural differences in ethics, 86–88, 115
Cummins Engine Company, 6, 102

Dalrymple, D.J., 42
Darden, W.R., 71
Day, R.L., 56

Del Monte Corporation, 86
Delbecq, A.L., 44
Diamond, S.A., 59–60
Difference principle, 20–22
Dodge, H.R., 42
Drucker, Peter F., 6
Dubinsky, Alan J., 42–44, 46, 49, 51–52, 55, 71, 74

Electrical manufacturers, 75–76
Epstein, Edwin M., 2
Ethical absolutism, 27
Ethical conflict, 41–42, 97
Ethical dilemmas: defined, 97; resolution of, 22
Ethical duties, 14–16
Ethical frameworks, 14–22, 27; value of, 22
Ethical guidelines: for advertising, 36–39; for multinational marketing, 94–95; for pricing, 79–81
Ethical relativism, 27
Ethics: difficulties with, 2; and individual responsibility, 98; and job satisfaction, 42; and the law, 4, 112, 115; need for research in, 5; and persuasion, 34–35; and rationalization, 3
Ethics committees, 102–103; advantages, 102; disadvantages, 103
Ethics scenarios, 10, 41, 89–91
Externalities, 98

Farmer, Richard N., 12
Feldman, Lawrence P., 2
Ferrell, O.C., 9, 13, 35–37, 71, 78, 100
Fisk, George, 13
Folding carton industry, 76–77
Ford, N.M., 42
Foreign Corrupt Practices Act of 1977, 85, 91, 98
Fox Importers, 93–94
FRAM, 29
Frey, C.J., 57, 61
Fritzsche, David J., 86
Frons, Marc, 35
Furash, E.E., 69
Futrell, C., 42, 47

Galbraith, John Kenneth, 33
Gallup, 2, 99

Gantrade Corporation, 86
Garrett, Thomas, 13–14, 17–19, 22, 24
Gelb, B.D., 55
General Electric, 76
General Motors, 149–156
Giant Foods, 157–164
Goldfield, E.D., 62
Greyser, Steven A., 35–36
Gustafson, D.H., 44
Gwin, John M., 42, 71, 74

Hawkins, D.I., 55, 62
Helfand, T., 71
Herman, Edward S., 6
Heublein, 139–148
Hollander, Jr., S., 57
Hunt, S.D., 46
Hunt, Shelby, D., 13

IBM, 78, 117–124
ITT, 135–136

Jacobs, Bruce A., 71, 75
John Paul II, 82
Johnson Wax, 125–128, 129–132
Justice principle, 88–89

Kaikati, Jack G., 98
Kehoe, William J., 71
Kelley, Eugene J., 9
Kerin, R.S., 46
Kinnear, T.C., 57, 61
Kizelbach, A.H., 9
Kramer, O.P., 43
Krugman, Dean, 35–36

Label, Wayne A., 98
Laczniak, Gene R., 9, 12, 27, 33, 42, 55, 71, 73, 94, 103, 104
Lawyer, John Q., 71, 75
Levitt, Theodore, 30, 32–33
Levy, M., 42, 44, 46, 49, 51–52
Liberty principle, 20–22
Lockheed Aircraft Corporation, 85
Lusch, Robert F., 12

M&Ms, 30–31
McClenahan, John, 71, 75
McMahon, T.F., 57
McMahon, Thomas V., 12
Maidenform, 27–28

Manipulation in advertising, 30, 32–34
Marketing ethics: consequences of, 97; costs of, 98
Marketing research ethics, 55–70; and client rights, 63–66; questionable practices in, 56; report writing, 67; research code of, 58; among research firms, 66–68; and respondant rights, 61–63
Mars, 30–31
Mertes, John E., 33
Miller, Edward A., 6
Miller, Mary S., 6
Minimax decision making, 20
Misrepresentation, 117
Moberg, Dennis J., 93
Models of ethical decision making, 23, 37, 92
Molander, E.A., 43
Monsanto, 102
Morgan, Fred W., 92
Mosaic law, 2
Munson, Howard, 103
Murphy, Patrick E., 9, 12, 33, 42, 55, 71, 73, 94

National Advertising Review Board (NARB), 29
Nestle, 98
Net social benefits approach, 93
Nominal group technique, 44
Norton Corporation, 102

Occupations and perceptions of honesty, 99
Original position, 20

Packard, Vance, 33
Patterson, James M., 12
Peterson, R.A., 46
Post, James E., 96
Pricing and ethics, 71–82; price fixing, 3–4, 75–77; need for research in, 78–79; intracompany pricing, 114
Privacy Act of 1974, 55
Privacy, the right of, 61–63
Product quality, 112
Product safety, 136
Profit, the concept of, 72–73
Proportionality framework, 17–19
Pruden, Henry, 12

Puffery, 33
Purcell, Theodore V., S.J., 80, 104

Quaker Oats, 101

Rawls, John, 12–14, 20–22, 24
Reciprocal dealing, 118
Reece, Bonnie, 35–36
Ricklefs, Roger, 3
Rights principle, 88
Robin, Donald P., 12, 27
Ross, William David, 13–14, 16, 22, 24
Rountree, W.D., 53
Rudelius, William, 9, 42–43, 49, 55, 71, 74, 78
Rules of ethics, thumbnail, 11
Russell, F.A., 42

Sabertehrani, M., 46
Sales management, determining ethical problems in selling, 43
Sam P. Wallace Company, 91
Sartorius, Rolf E., 14
Security and Exchange Commission (SEC), 4
Sethi, S. Prakash, 98
Sherman Antitrust Act, 75
Shuptrine, F.K., 55
Singer, E., 62
Singer, Peter, 14
Smith, J.G., 56
Social justice framework, 20–22
Sonnenfeld, Jeffrey, 71, 76–77
Sparkman, R.D., 46
Stanton, W.J., 42
Stasch, S.F., 47
Steckmest, Francis W., 77
Steiner, George, 2
Steiner, John, 2
Steiner, John F., 12
Sturdivant, Frederick D., 9, 71, 100

Teaching ethics, 6, 11, 79, 103–104
Technology, 113–114
Telemarketing, unethical, 61
Trawick, Fred, 71
Turk, Peter, 35
Tybout, A.M., 50

Unethical behavior, reasons for, 2–3, 77–78
Union Carbide Corporation, 86
Universal Product Codes, 79, 157–163
Upjohn Corporation, 89
U.S. Executive Office of the President, 61
Utilitarianism, 14, 88

Van De Ven, A.H., 44
Velasquez, Manuel, 73, 88, 93
Virginia Slims, 30, 32–34

Walker, O.C., 42
Wall Street Journal, 3–4

Walton, Clarence C., 12, 71, 77, 81
Weaver, K.M., 9, 36–37, 71, 78, 100
Westfall, R., 47
Westing, Howard J., 12
Westinghouse, 76
Whistle blowing, 102
Wilcox, J.B., 47
Williams, Oliver F., 72
Williams, Rev. Oliver F., 6
Wright, John S., 33

Zaltman, G., 56
Zey-Ferrell, Mary, 36

About the Contributors

Alan J. Dubinsky is a visiting associate professor of marketing at the University of Minnesota. He is a frequent contributor to academic journals including the *Journal of Retailing* and the *Journal of Business Ethics*. Previously, he was on the faculty of the University of Kentucky.

O.C. Ferrell is a professor of marketing at Texas A&M University. He is the coauthor of a leading marketing textbook—*Marketing: Basic Concepts and Decisions*. His writings about ethics have appeared in the *Journal of Marketing* and the *Journal of Advertising*.

David J. Fritzsche is a professor of marketing and chairman of the Managerial Sciences Department at the University of Nevada-Reno. His articles have appeared in the top scholarly journals including *Journal of Marketing Research* and *Academy of Managment Journal*. He was a faculty member at Illinois State University.

Del I. Hawkins is a professor of marketing at the University of Oregon. He is coauthor of *Marketing Research: Measurement and Method* and *Consumer Behavior*. He also serves as a consultant to several major corporations.

William J. Kehoe is a professor of marketing at the University of Virginia. Currently, he serves as associate dean for external affairs for the McIntire School of Commerce there. His articles have appeared in the *Journal of Marketing* and *Journal of Bank Research*.

T.R. Martin is a professor of management at Marquette University. He is the former dean of the College of Business Administration at Marquette and past president of Beta Gamma Sigma. He is the author of a number of scholarly articles and editor of *Stewardship: The Corporation and The Individual*.

Donald S. Tull is a professor of marketing at the University of Oregon. He is the coauthor of three texts in the field of marketing research. He has contributed articles to many journals including the *Journal of Marketing Research*.

About the Editors

Gene R. Laczniak is professor of business and chairman, Department of Marketing at Marquette University. Dr. Laczniak earned the Ph.D. in business administration at the University of Wisconsin-Madison. His primary research interests focus on the social influence of marketing activities on society as well as marketing strategy. Dr. Laczniak has published over fifty articles and papers. His works have appeared in the *Journal of Marketing, Journal of Retailing, Journalism Quarterly*, and *Journal of Consumer Affairs*. He is active in the American Marketing Association and has worked as a marketing research specialist for the U.S. Treasury Department and a NASA Biomedical Applications Team.

Patrick E. Murphy is presently associate professor of marketing at the University of Notre Dame. Dr. Murphy earned the Ph.D. in business administration from the University of Houston. His primary research interests focus on the application of marketing to nonprofit organizations as well as ethical and public policy issues facing business. He has published numerous articles in scholarly journals such as the *Journal of Marketing, Journal of Consumer Research*, and *Journal of Macromarketing* and is the co-author of a recently published textbook, *Marketing* (Scott Foresman, 1985). He served as vice-president of the Marketing Education Division of the American Marketing Association during 1985–86 and has worked in the Bureau of Consumer protection of the Federal Trade Commission.